Walt Disney's Donald Duck

• In a Minor Key •

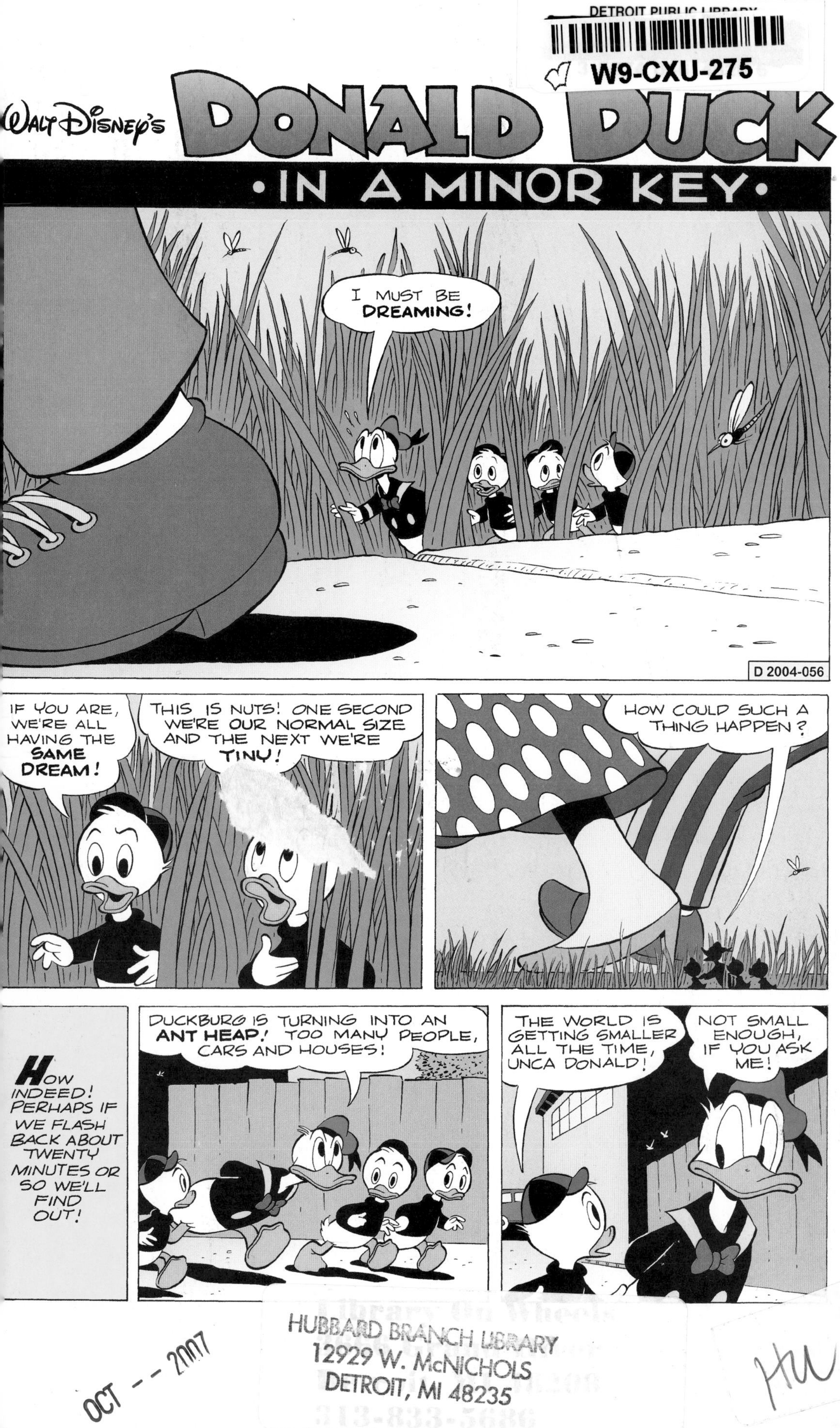
I MUST BE DREAMING!
D 2004-056
IF YOU ARE, WE'RE ALL HAVING THE SAME DREAM!
THIS IS NUTS! ONE SECOND WE'RE OUR NORMAL SIZE AND THE NEXT WE'RE TINY!
HOW COULD SUCH A THING HAPPEN?
HOW INDEED! PERHAPS IF WE FLASH BACK ABOUT TWENTY MINUTES OR SO WE'LL FIND OUT!
DUCKBURG IS TURNING INTO AN ANT HEAP! TOO MANY PEOPLE, CARS AND HOUSES!
THE WORLD IS GETTING SMALLER ALL THE TIME, UNCA DONALD!
NOT SMALL ENOUGH, IF YOU ASK ME!

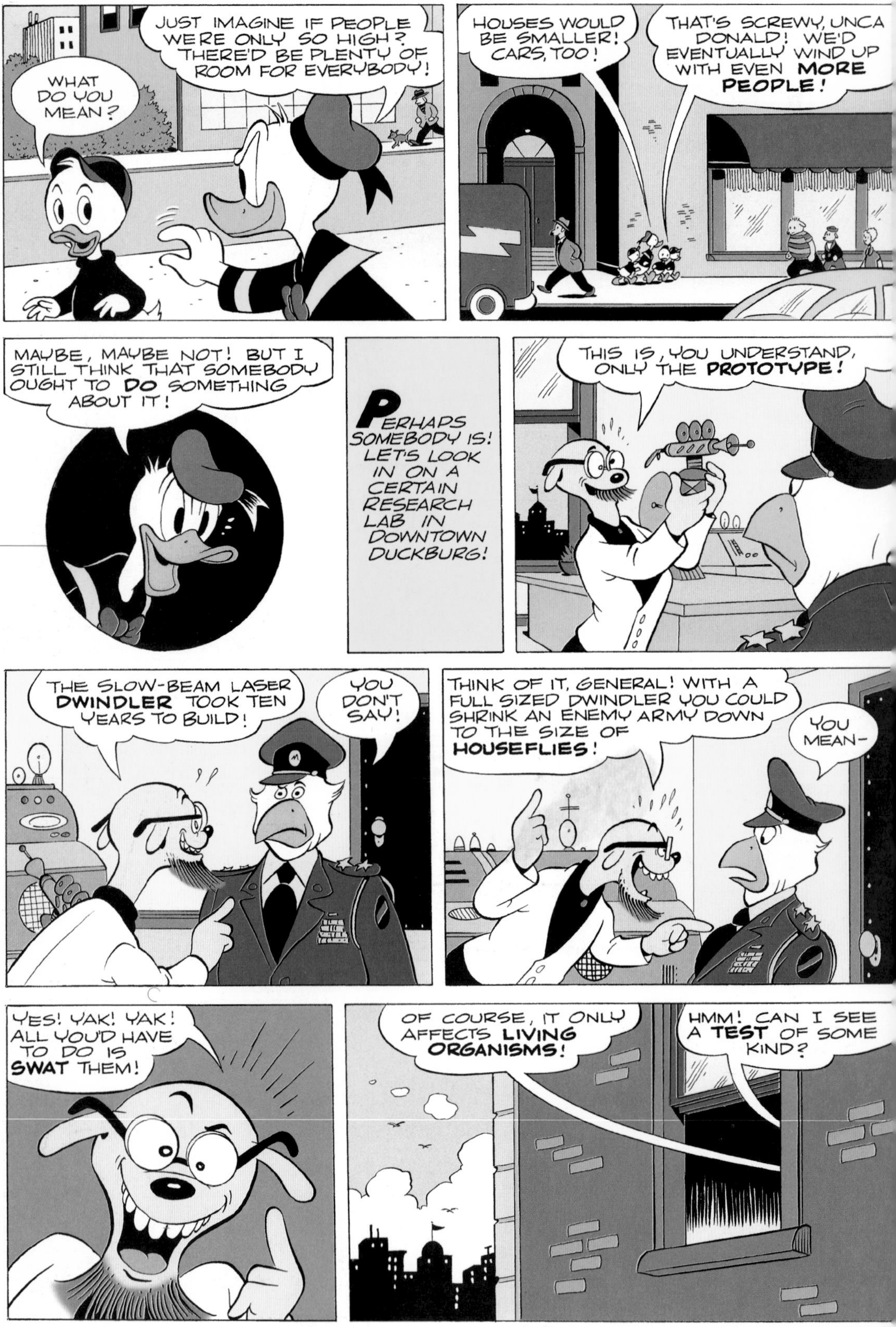
WHAT DO YOU MEAN?
JUST IMAGINE IF PEOPLE WERE ONLY SO HIGH? THERE'D BE PLENTY OF ROOM FOR EVERYBODY!
HOUSES WOULD BE SMALLER! CARS, TOO!
THAT'S SCREWY, UNCA DONALD! WE'D EVENTUALLY WIND UP WITH EVEN MORE PEOPLE!
MAYBE, MAYBE NOT! BUT I STILL THINK THAT SOMEBODY OUGHT TO DO SOMETHING ABOUT IT!
PERHAPS SOMEBODY IS! LET'S LOOK IN ON A CERTAIN RESEARCH LAB IN DOWNTOWN DUCKBURG!
THIS IS, YOU UNDERSTAND, ONLY THE PROTOTYPE!
THE SLOW-BEAM LASER DWINDLER TOOK TEN YEARS TO BUILD!
YOU DON'T SAY!
THINK OF IT, GENERAL! WITH A FULL SIZED DWINDLER YOU COULD SHRINK AN ENEMY ARMY DOWN TO THE SIZE OF HOUSEFLIES!
YOU MEAN-
YES! YAK! YAK! ALL YOU'D HAVE TO DO IS SWAT THEM!
OF COURSE, IT ONLY AFFECTS LIVING ORGANISMS!
HMM! CAN I SEE A TEST OF SOME KIND?

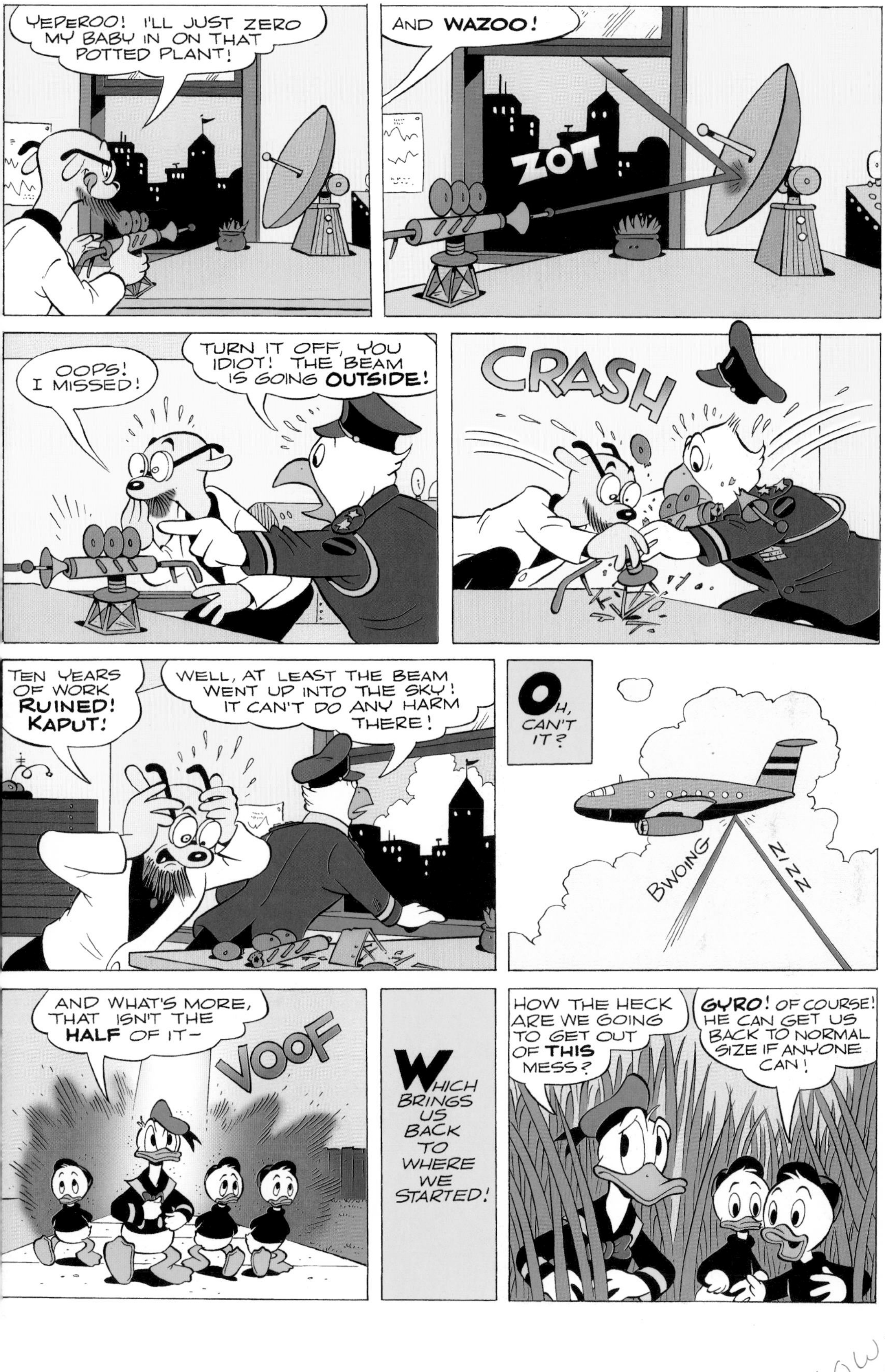

YEPEROO! I'LL JUST ZERO MY BABY IN ON THAT POTTED PLANT!
AND WAZOO!
ZOT
OOPS! I MISSED!
TURN IT OFF, YOU IDIOT! THE BEAM IS GOING OUTSIDE!
CRASH
TEN YEARS OF WORK RUINED! KAPUT!
WELL, AT LEAST THE BEAM WENT UP INTO THE SKY! IT CAN'T DO ANY HARM THERE!
OH, CAN'T IT?
BWOING
ZIZZ
AND WHAT'S MORE, THAT ISN'T THE HALF OF IT–
VOOF
WHICH BRINGS US BACK TO WHERE WE STARTED!
HOW THE HECK ARE WE GOING TO GET OUT OF THIS MESS?
GYRO! OF COURSE! HE CAN GET US BACK TO NORMAL SIZE IF ANYONE CAN!

LOW-50

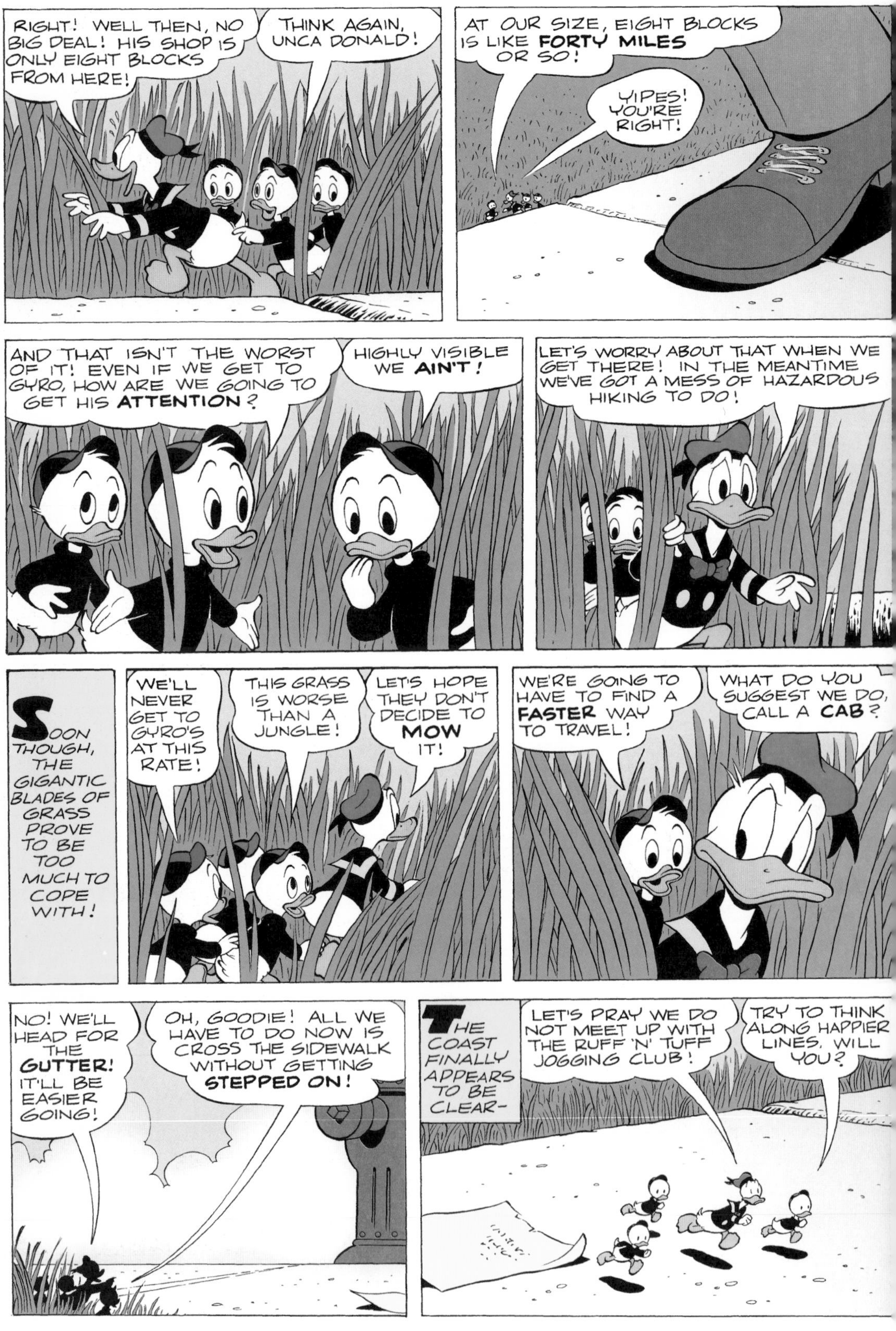
RIGHT! WELL THEN, NO BIG DEAL! HIS SHOP IS ONLY EIGHT BLOCKS FROM HERE!
THINK AGAIN, UNCA DONALD!
AT OUR SIZE, EIGHT BLOCKS IS LIKE FORTY MILES OR SO!
YIPES! YOU'RE RIGHT!
AND THAT ISN'T THE WORST OF IT! EVEN IF WE GET TO GYRO, HOW ARE WE GOING TO GET HIS ATTENTION?
HIGHLY VISIBLE WE AIN'T!
LET'S WORRY ABOUT THAT WHEN WE GET THERE! IN THE MEANTIME WE'VE GOT A MESS OF HAZARDOUS HIKING TO DO!
SOON THOUGH, THE GIGANTIC BLADES OF GRASS PROVE TO BE TOO MUCH TO COPE WITH!
WE'LL NEVER GET TO GYRO'S AT THIS RATE!
THIS GRASS IS WORSE THAN A JUNGLE!
LET'S HOPE THEY DON'T DECIDE TO MOW IT!
WE'RE GOING TO HAVE TO FIND A FASTER WAY TO TRAVEL!
WHAT DO YOU SUGGEST WE DO, CALL A CAB?
NO! WE'LL HEAD FOR THE GUTTER! IT'LL BE EASIER GOING!
OH, GOODIE! ALL WE HAVE TO DO NOW IS CROSS THE SIDEWALK WITHOUT GETTING STEPPED ON!
THE COAST FINALLY APPEARS TO BE CLEAR-
LET'S PRAY WE DO NOT MEET UP WITH THE RUFF 'N' TUFF JOGGING CLUB!
TRY TO THINK ALONG HAPPIER LINES, WILL YOU?

35674046146206

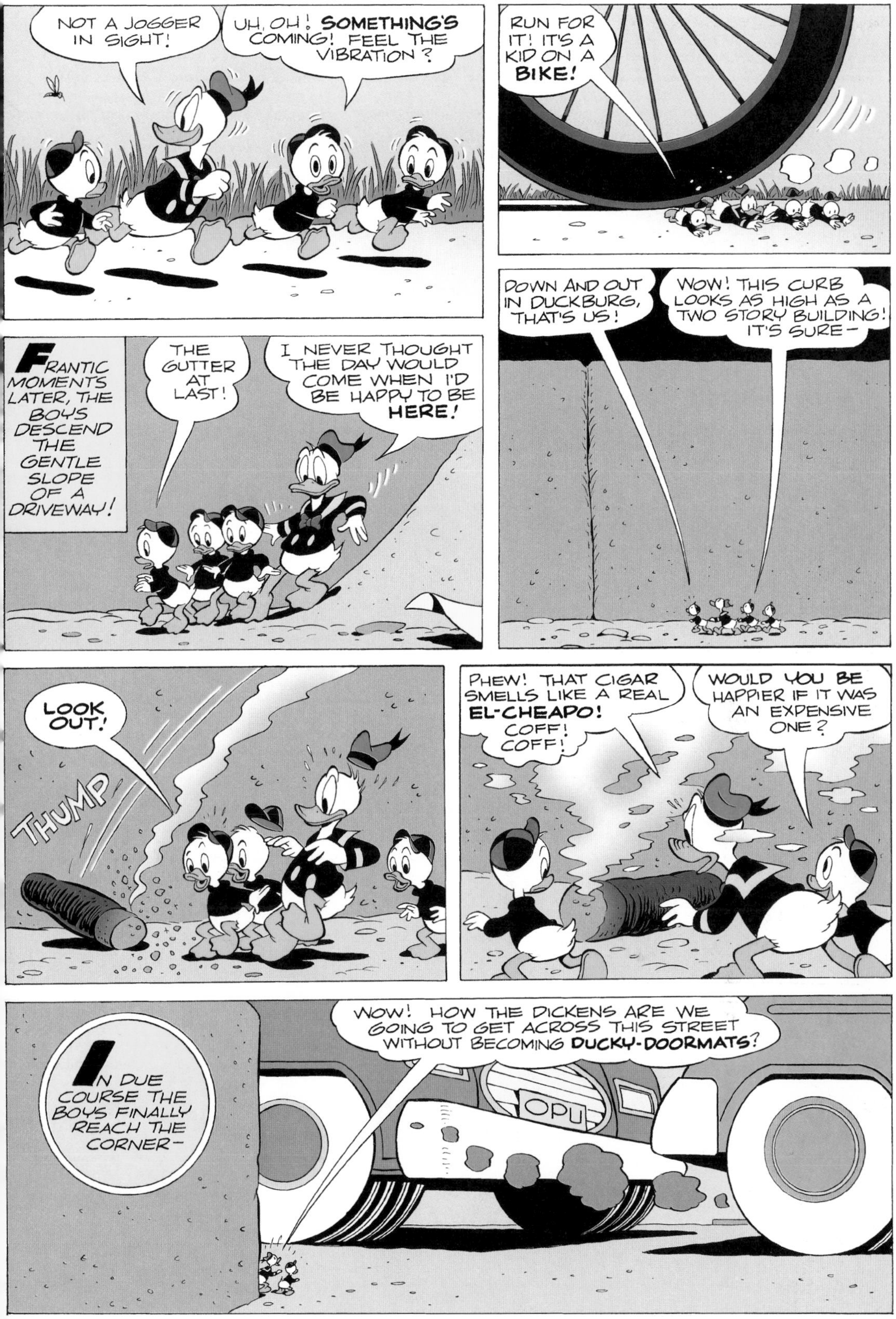
NOT A JOGGER IN SIGHT!
UH, OH! SOMETHING'S COMING! FEEL THE VIBRATION?
RUN FOR IT! IT'S A KID ON A BIKE!
FRANTIC MOMENTS LATER, THE BOYS DESCEND THE GENTLE SLOPE OF A DRIVEWAY!
THE GUTTER AT LAST!
I NEVER THOUGHT THE DAY WOULD COME WHEN I'D BE HAPPY TO BE HERE!
DOWN AND OUT IN DUCKBURG, THAT'S US!
WOW! THIS CURB LOOKS AS HIGH AS A TWO STORY BUILDING! IT'S SURE—
LOOK OUT!
THUMP
PHEW! THAT CIGAR SMELLS LIKE A REAL EL-CHEAPO! COFF! COFF!
WOULD YOU BE HAPPIER IF IT WAS AN EXPENSIVE ONE?
IN DUE COURSE THE BOYS FINALLY REACH THE CORNER—
WOW! HOW THE DICKENS ARE WE GOING TO GET ACROSS THIS STREET WITHOUT BECOMING DUCKY-DOORMATS?
OPU

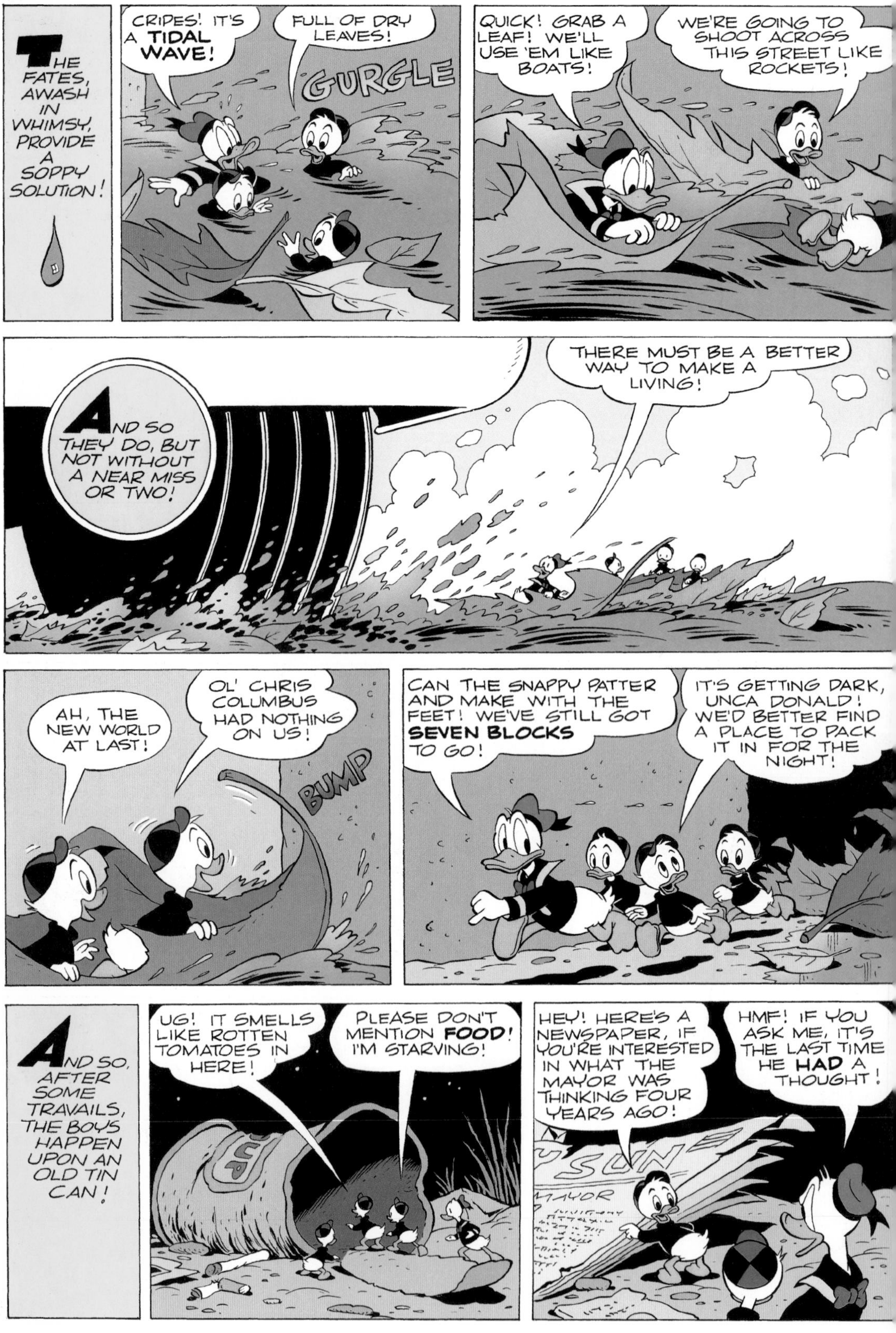

THE FATES, AWASH IN WHIMSY, PROVIDE A SOPPY SOLUTION!
CRIPES! IT'S A TIDAL WAVE!
FULL OF DRY LEAVES!
GURGLE
QUICK! GRAB A LEAF! WE'LL USE 'EM LIKE BOATS!
WE'RE GOING TO SHOOT ACROSS THIS STREET LIKE ROCKETS!
AND SO THEY DO, BUT NOT WITHOUT A NEAR MISS OR TWO!
THERE MUST BE A BETTER WAY TO MAKE A LIVING!
AH, THE NEW WORLD AT LAST!
OL' CHRIS COLUMBUS HAD NOTHING ON US!
BUMP
CAN THE SNAPPY PATTER AND MAKE WITH THE FEET! WE'VE STILL GOT SEVEN BLOCKS TO GO!
IT'S GETTING DARK, UNCA DONALD! WE'D BETTER FIND A PLACE TO PACK IT IN FOR THE NIGHT!
AND SO, AFTER SOME TRAVAILS, THE BOYS HAPPEN UPON AN OLD TIN CAN!
UG! IT SMELLS LIKE ROTTEN TOMATOES IN HERE!
PLEASE DON'T MENTION FOOD! I'M STARVING!
HEY! HERE'S A NEWSPAPER, IF YOU'RE INTERESTED IN WHAT THE MAYOR WAS THINKING FOUR YEARS AGO!
HMF! IF YOU ASK ME, IT'S THE LAST TIME HE HAD A THOUGHT!
SUN
MAYOR

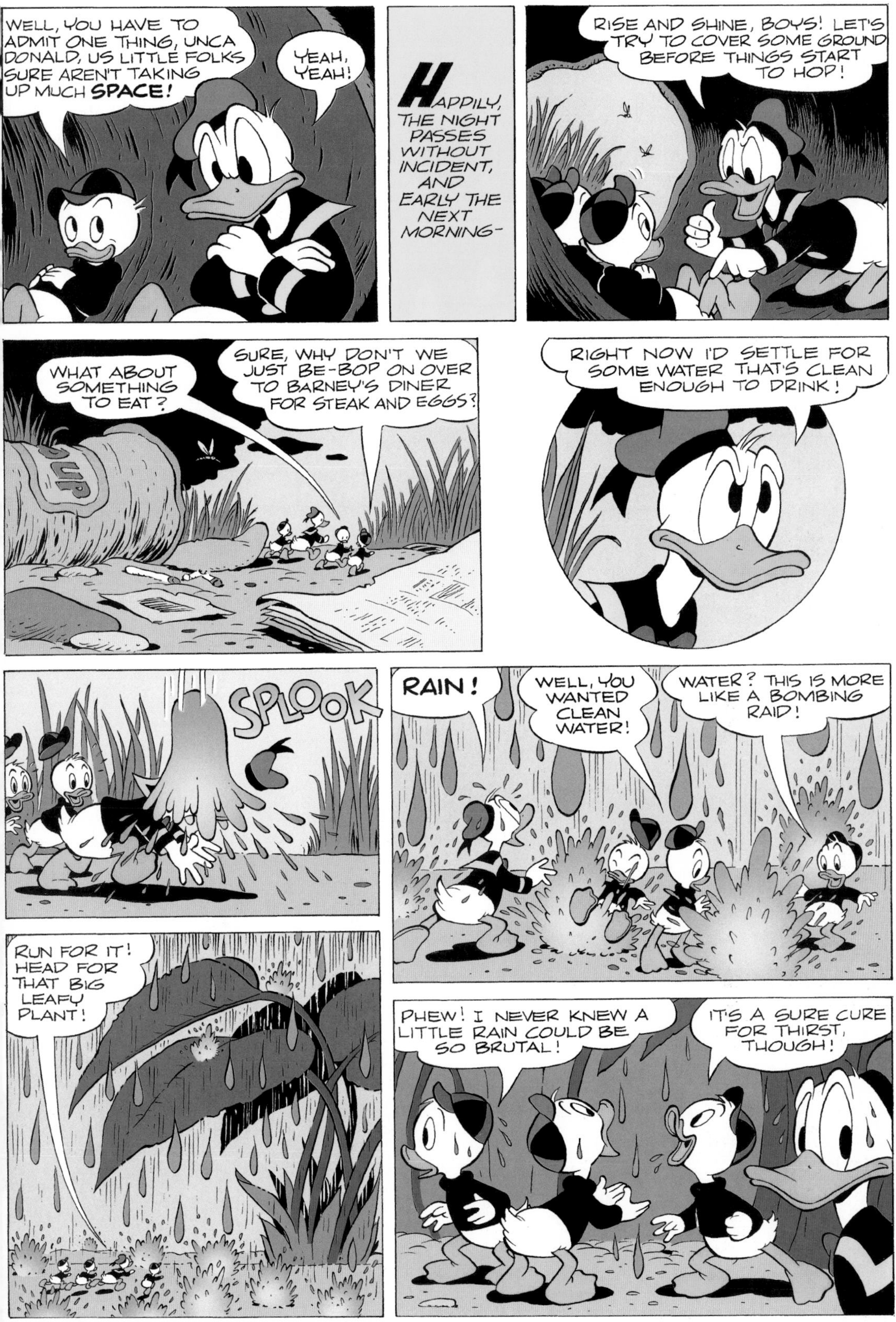
WELL, YOU HAVE TO ADMIT ONE THING, UNCA DONALD, US LITTLE FOLKS SURE AREN'T TAKING UP MUCH **SPACE**!
YEAH, YEAH!
HAPPILY, THE NIGHT PASSES WITHOUT INCIDENT, AND EARLY THE NEXT MORNING–
RISE AND SHINE, BOYS! LET'S TRY TO COVER SOME GROUND BEFORE THINGS START TO HOP!
WHAT ABOUT SOMETHING TO EAT?
SURE, WHY DON'T WE JUST BE-BOP ON OVER TO BARNEY'S DINER FOR STEAK AND EGGS?
RIGHT NOW I'D SETTLE FOR SOME WATER THAT'S CLEAN ENOUGH TO DRINK!
SPLOOK
RAIN!
WELL, YOU WANTED CLEAN WATER!
WATER? THIS IS MORE LIKE A BOMBING RAID!
RUN FOR IT! HEAD FOR THAT BIG LEAFY PLANT!
PHEW! I NEVER KNEW A LITTLE RAIN COULD BE SO BRUTAL!
IT'S A SURE CURE FOR THIRST, THOUGH!

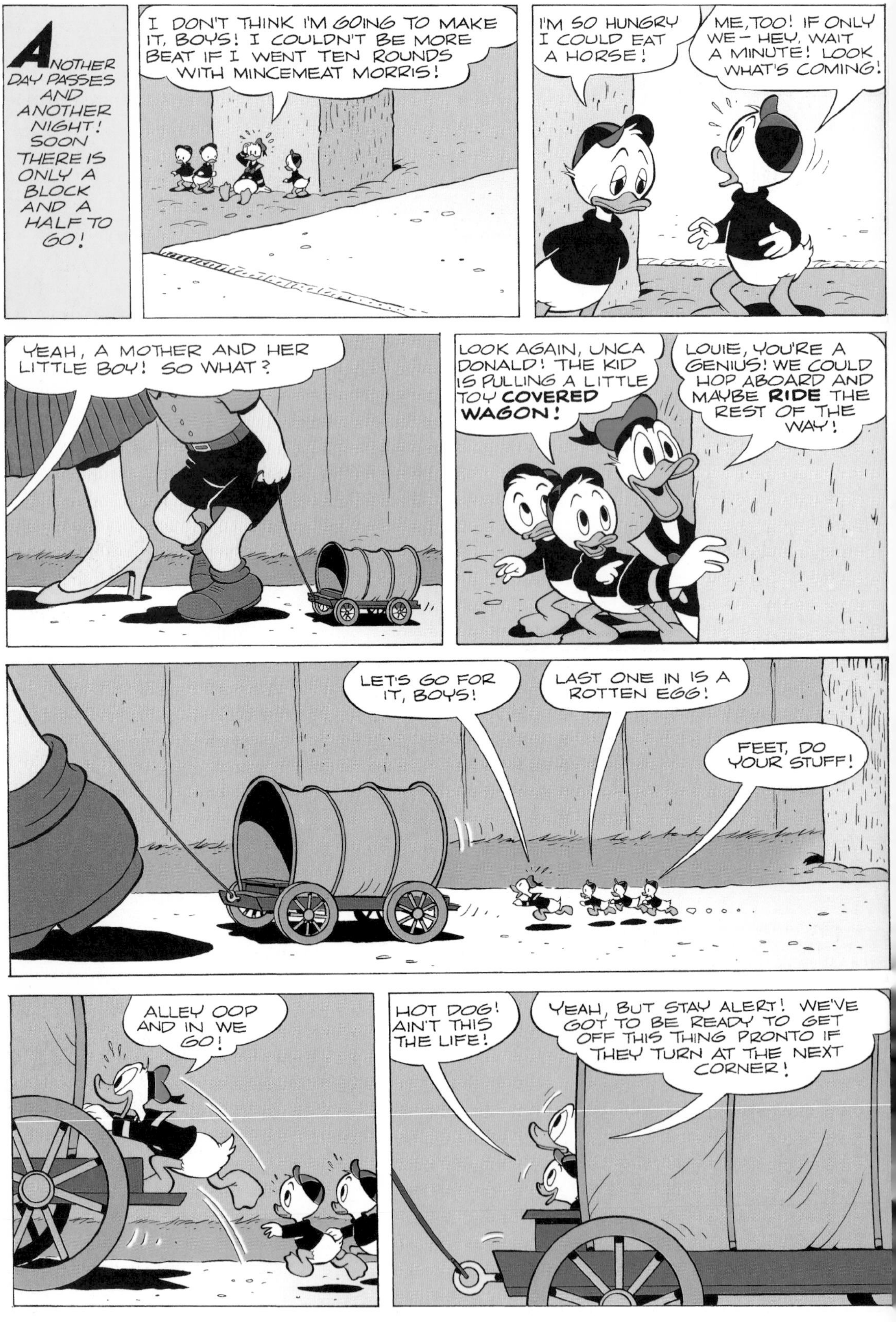
ANOTHER DAY PASSES AND ANOTHER NIGHT! SOON THERE IS ONLY A BLOCK AND A HALF TO GO!
I DON'T THINK I'M GOING TO MAKE IT, BOYS! I COULDN'T BE MORE BEAT IF I WENT TEN ROUNDS WITH MINCEMEAT MORRIS!
I'M SO HUNGRY I COULD EAT A HORSE!
ME, TOO! IF ONLY WE — HEY, WAIT A MINUTE! LOOK WHAT'S COMING!
YEAH, A MOTHER AND HER LITTLE BOY! SO WHAT?
LOOK AGAIN, UNCA DONALD! THE KID IS PULLING A LITTLE TOY COVERED WAGON!
LOUIE, YOU'RE A GENIUS! WE COULD HOP ABOARD AND MAYBE RIDE THE REST OF THE WAY!
LET'S GO FOR IT, BOYS!
LAST ONE IN IS A ROTTEN EGG!
FEET, DO YOUR STUFF!
ALLEY OOP AND IN WE GO!
HOT DOG! AIN'T THIS THE LIFE!
YEAH, BUT STAY ALERT! WE'VE GOT TO BE READY TO GET OFF THIS THING PRONTO IF THEY TURN AT THE NEXT CORNER!

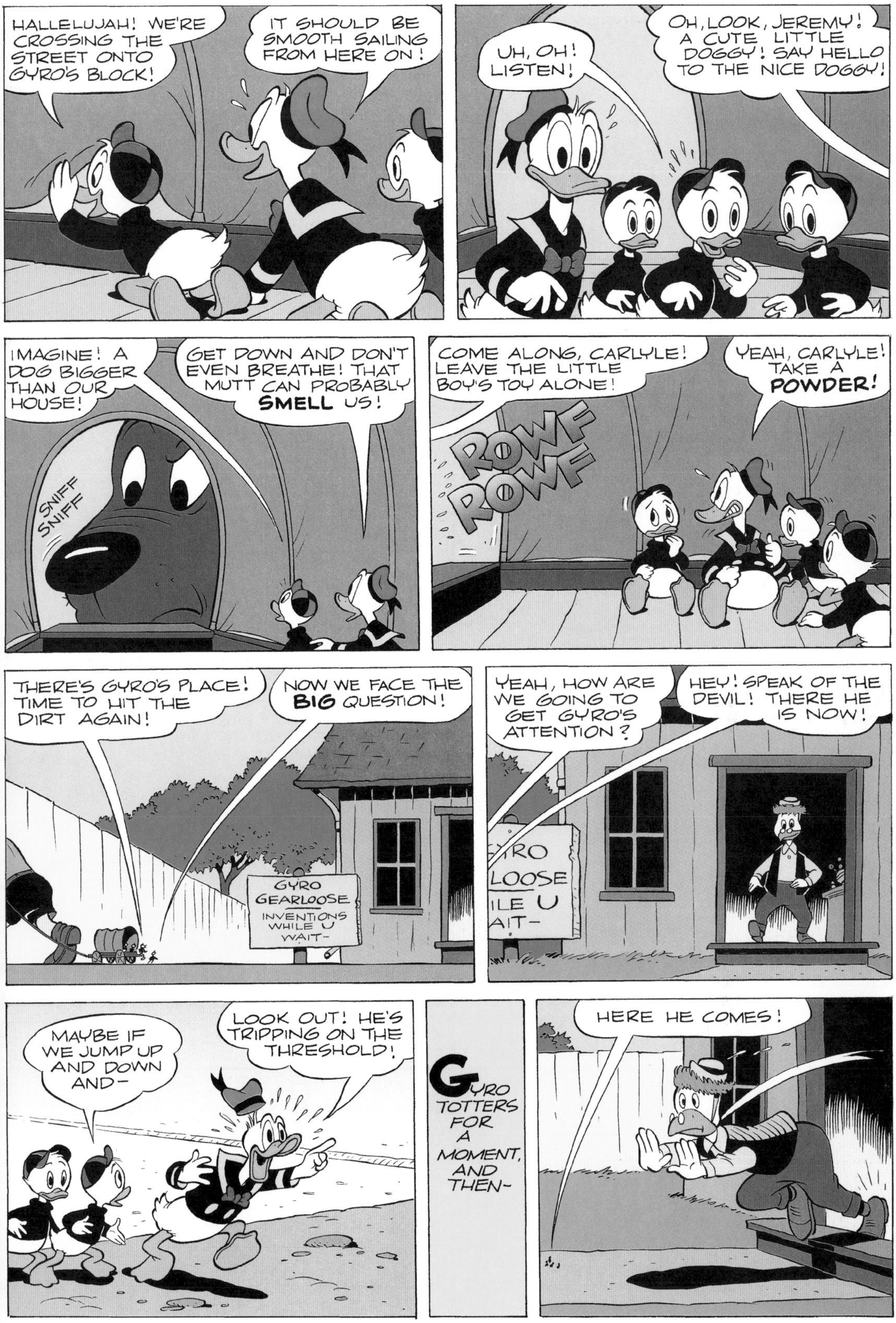
HALLELUJAH! WE'RE CROSSING THE STREET ONTO GYRO'S BLOCK!
IT SHOULD BE SMOOTH SAILING FROM HERE ON!
UH, OH! LISTEN!
OH, LOOK, JEREMY! A CUTE LITTLE DOGGY! SAY HELLO TO THE NICE DOGGY!
IMAGINE! A DOG BIGGER THAN OUR HOUSE!
GET DOWN AND DON'T EVEN BREATHE! THAT MUTT CAN PROBABLY SMELL US!
SNIFF SNIFF
COME ALONG, CARLYLE! LEAVE THE LITTLE BOY'S TOY ALONE!
YEAH, CARLYLE! TAKE A POWDER!
ROWF ROWF
THERE'S GYRO'S PLACE! TIME TO HIT THE DIRT AGAIN!
NOW WE FACE THE BIG QUESTION!
GYRO GEARLOOSE
INVENTIONS WHILE U WAIT-
YEAH, HOW ARE WE GOING TO GET GYRO'S ATTENTION?
HEY! SPEAK OF THE DEVIL! THERE HE IS NOW!
YRO LOOSE ILE U AIT-
MAYBE IF WE JUMP UP AND DOWN AND-
LOOK OUT! HE'S TRIPPING ON THE THRESHOLD!
GYRO TOTTERS FOR A MOMENT, AND THEN-
HERE HE COMES!

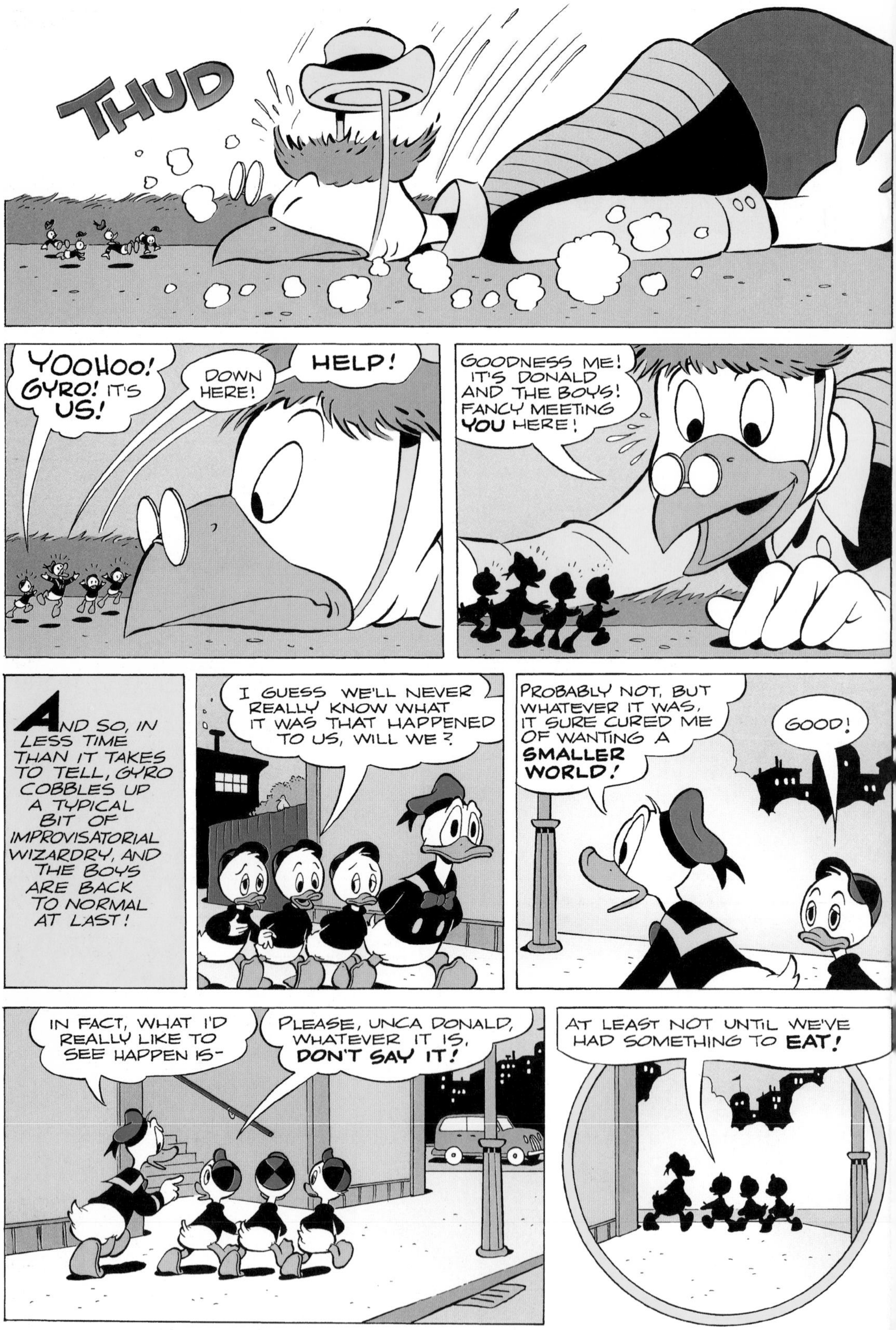
THUD
YOOHOO! GYRO! IT'S US!
DOWN HERE!
HELP!
GOODNESS ME! IT'S DONALD AND THE BOYS! FANCY MEETING YOU HERE!
AND SO, IN LESS TIME THAN IT TAKES TO TELL, GYRO COBBLES UP A TYPICAL BIT OF IMPROVISATORIAL WIZARDRY, AND THE BOYS ARE BACK TO NORMAL AT LAST!
I GUESS WE'LL NEVER REALLY KNOW WHAT IT WAS THAT HAPPENED TO US, WILL WE?
PROBABLY NOT, BUT WHATEVER IT WAS, IT SURE CURED ME OF WANTING A SMALLER WORLD!
GOOD!
IN FACT, WHAT I'D REALLY LIKE TO SEE HAPPEN IS-
PLEASE, UNCA DONALD, WHATEVER IT IS, DON'T SAY IT!
AT LEAST NOT UNTIL WE'VE HAD SOMETHING TO EAT!

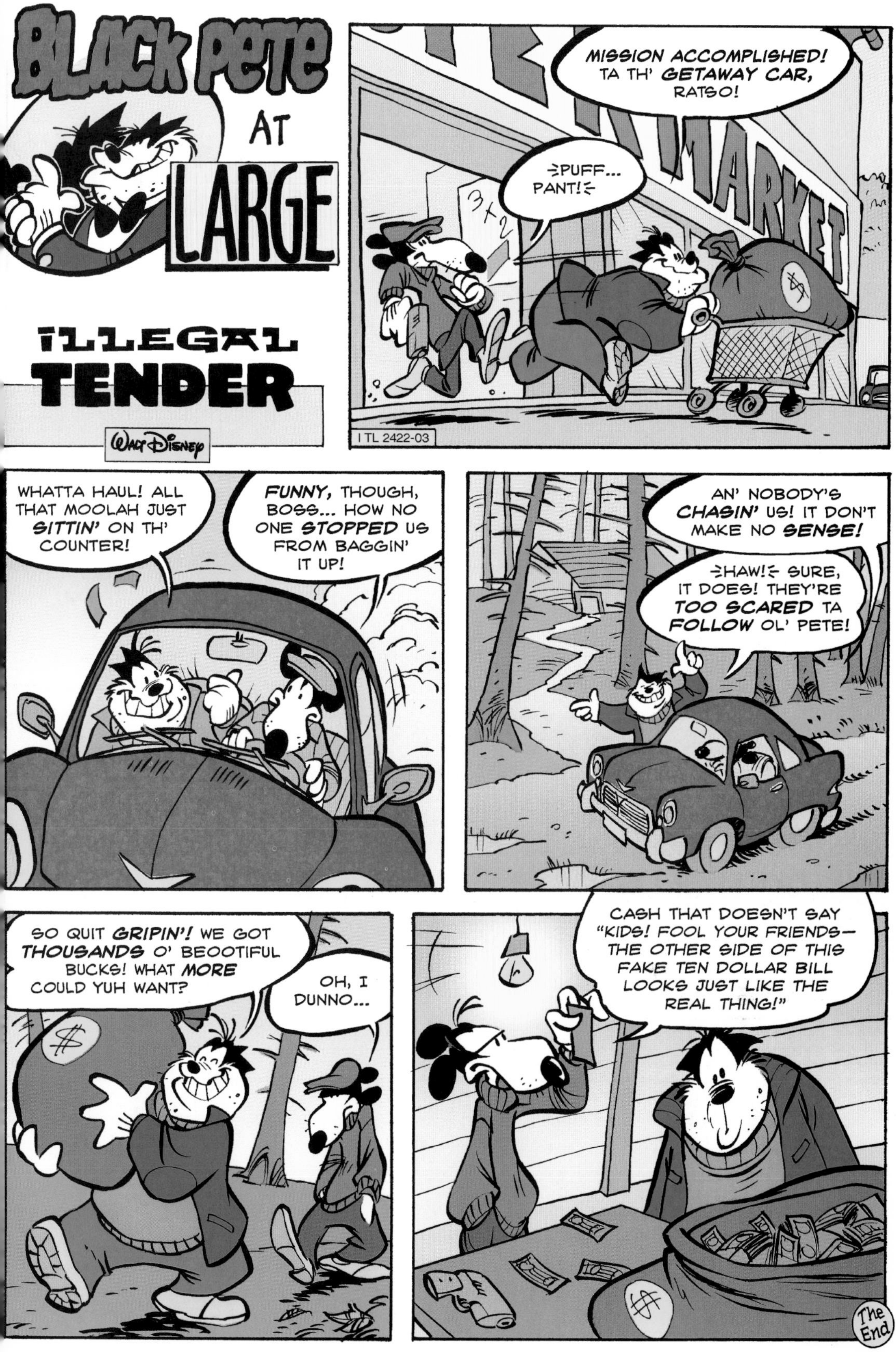
BLACK PETE AT LARGE
ILLEGAL TENDER
WALT DISNEY
MISSION ACCOMPLISHED! TA TH' GETAWAY CAR, RATSO!
≑PUFF... PANT!≑
MARKET
I TL 2422-03
WHATTA HAUL! ALL THAT MOOLAH JUST SITTIN' ON TH' COUNTER!
FUNNY, THOUGH, BOSS... HOW NO ONE STOPPED US FROM BAGGIN' IT UP!
AN' NOBODY'S CHASIN' US! IT DON'T MAKE NO SENSE!
≑HAW!≑ SURE, IT DOES! THEY'RE TOO SCARED TA FOLLOW OL' PETE!
SO QUIT GRIPIN'! WE GOT THOUSANDS O' BEOOTIFUL BUCKS! WHAT MORE COULD YUH WANT?
OH, I DUNNO...
CASH THAT DOESN'T SAY "KIDS! FOOL YOUR FRIENDS— THE OTHER SIDE OF THIS FAKE TEN DOLLAR BILL LOOKS JUST LIKE THE REAL THING!"
The End

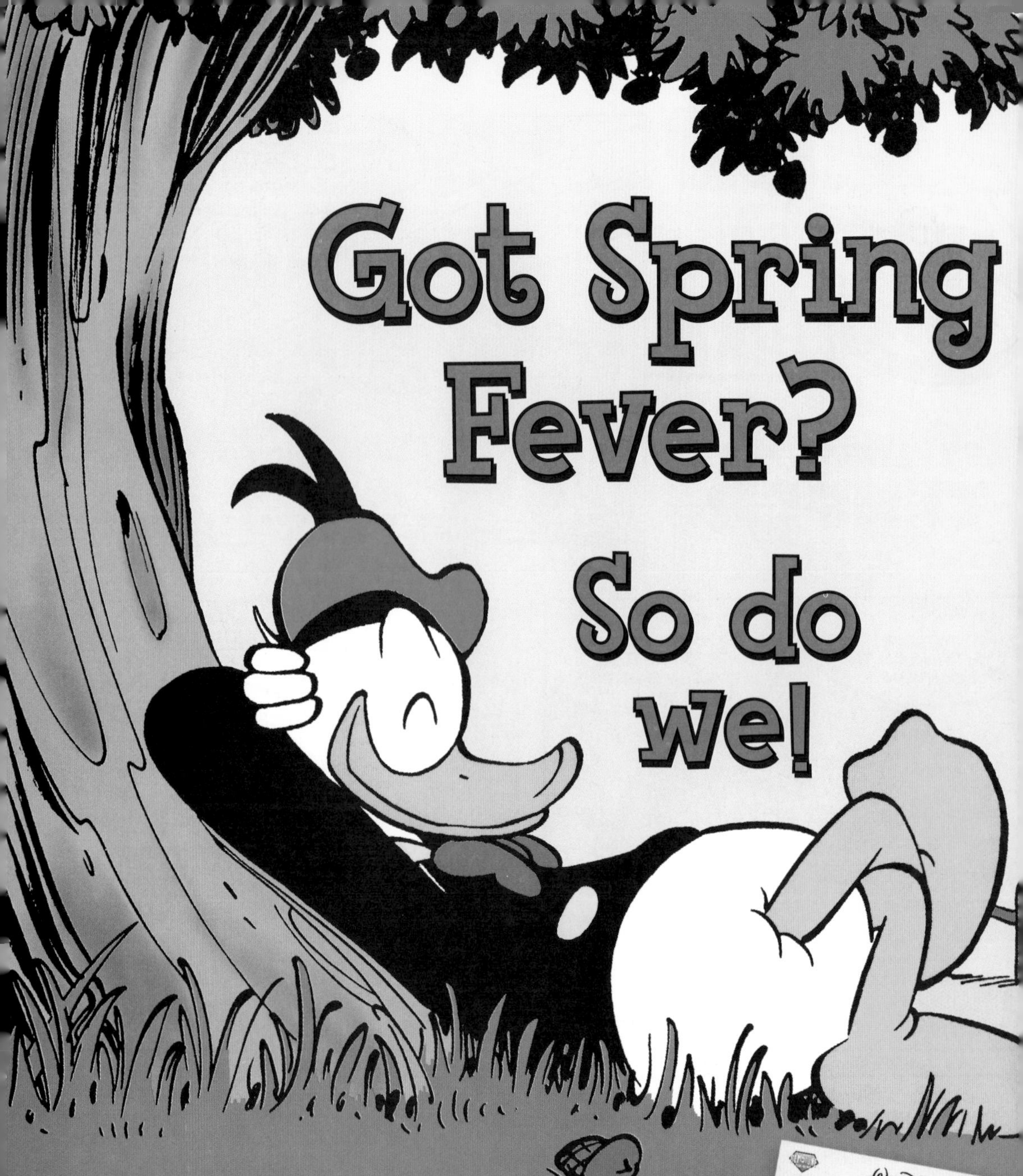
Got Spring Fever?
So do we!

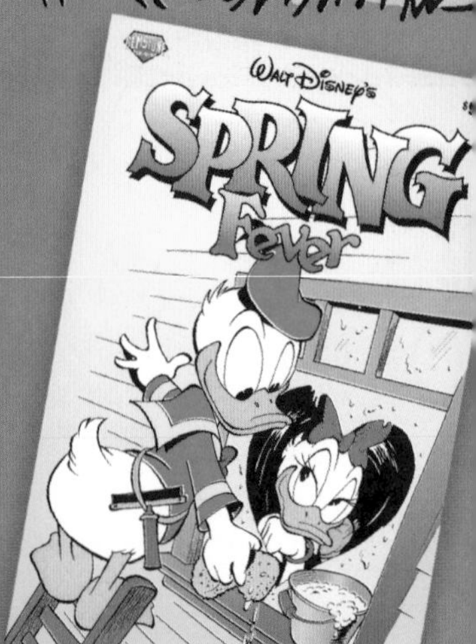
Walt Disney's
Spring
Fever

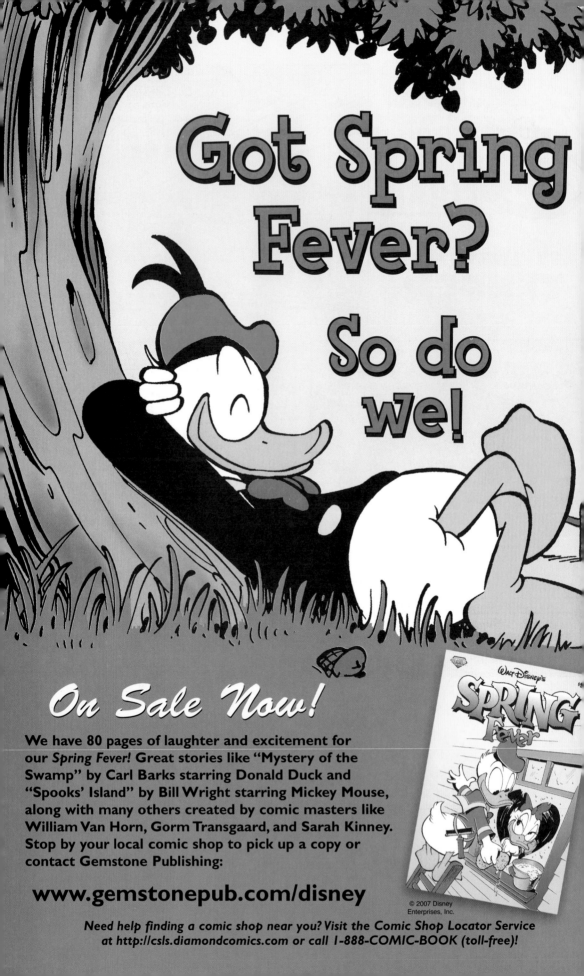

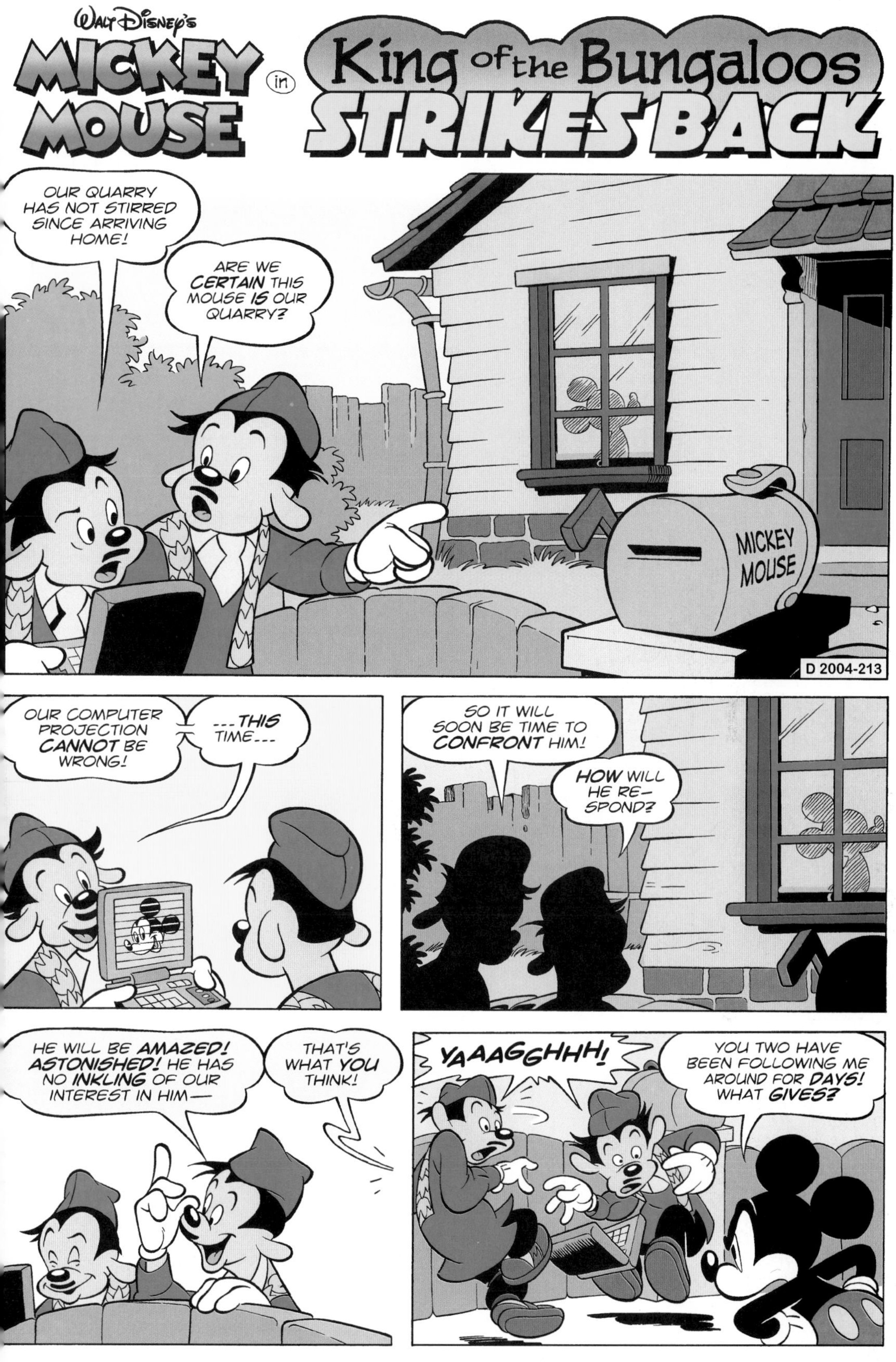
WALT DISNEY'S
MICKEY MOUSE
in
King of the Bungaloos
STRIKES BACK
OUR QUARRY HAS NOT STIRRED SINCE ARRIVING HOME!
ARE WE CERTAIN THIS MOUSE IS OUR QUARRY?
MICKEY MOUSE
D 2004-213
OUR COMPUTER PROJECTION CANNOT BE WRONG!
---THIS TIME---
SO IT WILL SOON BE TIME TO CONFRONT HIM!
HOW WILL HE RE-SPOND?
HE WILL BE AMAZED! ASTONISHED! HE HAS NO INKLING OF OUR INTEREST IN HIM—
THAT'S WHAT YOU THINK!
YAAAGGHHH!
YOU TWO HAVE BEEN FOLLOWING ME AROUND FOR DAYS! WHAT GIVES?

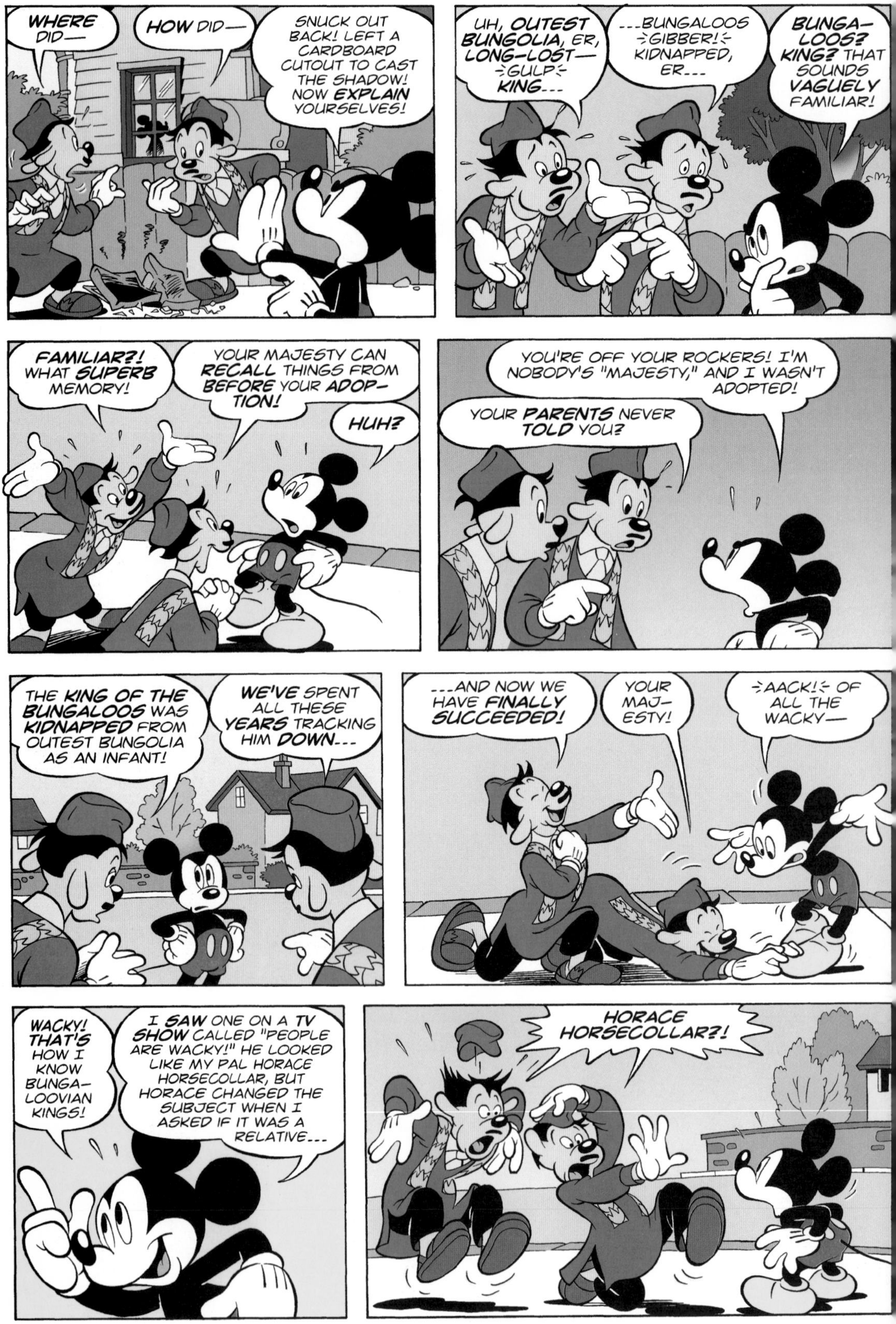
WHERE DID—
HOW DID—
SNUCK OUT BACK! LEFT A CARDBOARD CUTOUT TO CAST THE SHADOW! NOW EXPLAIN YOURSELVES!
UH, OUTEST BUNGOLIA, ER, LONG-LOST— GULP KING---
---BUNGALOOS GIBBER! KIDNAPPED, ER---
BUNGA-LOOS? KING? THAT SOUNDS VAGUELY FAMILIAR!
FAMILIAR?! WHAT SUPERB MEMORY!
YOUR MAJESTY CAN RECALL THINGS FROM BEFORE YOUR ADOP-TION!
HUH?
YOU'RE OFF YOUR ROCKERS! I'M NOBODY'S "MAJESTY," AND I WASN'T ADOPTED!
YOUR PARENTS NEVER TOLD YOU?
THE KING OF THE BUNGALOOS WAS KIDNAPPED FROM OUTEST BUNGOLIA AS AN INFANT!
WE'VE SPENT ALL THESE YEARS TRACKING HIM DOWN---
---AND NOW WE HAVE FINALLY SUCCEEDED!
YOUR MAJ-ESTY!
AACK! OF ALL THE WACKY—
WACKY! THAT'S HOW I KNOW BUNGA-LOOVIAN KINGS!
I SAW ONE ON A TV SHOW CALLED "PEOPLE ARE WACKY!" HE LOOKED LIKE MY PAL HORACE HORSECOLLAR, BUT HORACE CHANGED THE SUBJECT WHEN I ASKED IF IT WAS A RELATIVE---
HORACE HORSECOLLAR?!

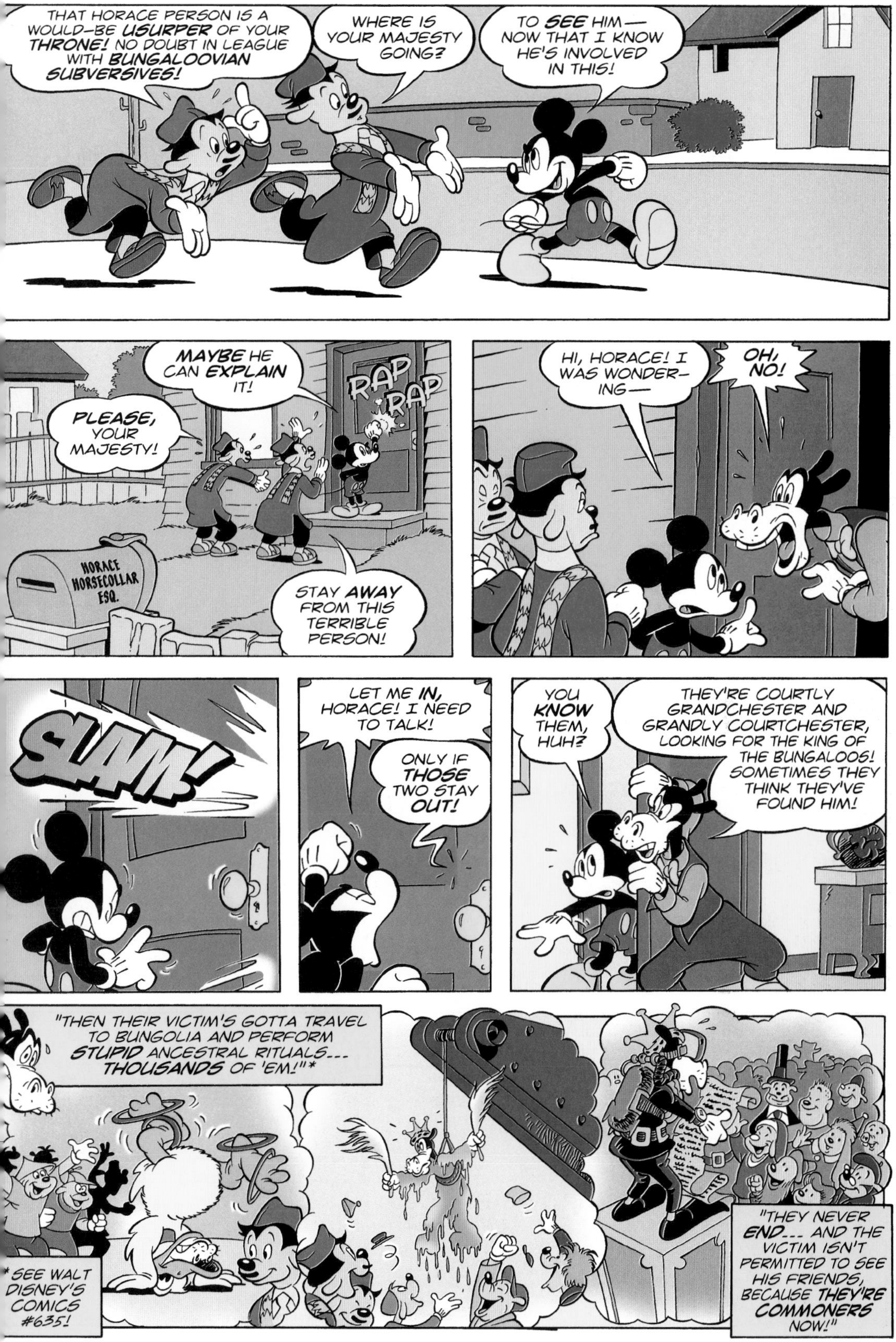

THAT HORACE PERSON IS A WOULD-BE USURPER OF YOUR THRONE! NO DOUBT IN LEAGUE WITH BUNGALOOVIAN SUBVERSIVES!
WHERE IS YOUR MAJESTY GOING?
TO SEE HIM— NOW THAT I KNOW HE'S INVOLVED IN THIS!
PLEASE, YOUR MAJESTY!
MAYBE HE CAN EXPLAIN IT!
RAP RAP
HORACE HORSECOLLAR ESQ.
STAY AWAY FROM THIS TERRIBLE PERSON!
HI, HORACE! I WAS WONDER-ING—
OH, NO!
SLAM!
LET ME IN, HORACE! I NEED TO TALK!
ONLY IF THOSE TWO STAY OUT!
YOU KNOW THEM, HUH?
THEY'RE COURTLY GRANDCHESTER AND GRANDLY COURTCHESTER, LOOKING FOR THE KING OF THE BUNGALOOS! SOMETIMES THEY THINK THEY'VE FOUND HIM!
"THEN THEIR VICTIM'S GOTTA TRAVEL TO BUNGOLIA AND PERFORM STUPID ANCESTRAL RITUALS--- THOUSANDS OF 'EM!"*
*SEE WALT DISNEY'S COMICS #635!
"THEY NEVER END--- AND THE VICTIM ISN'T PERMITTED TO SEE HIS FRIENDS, BECAUSE THEY'RE COMMONERS NOW!"

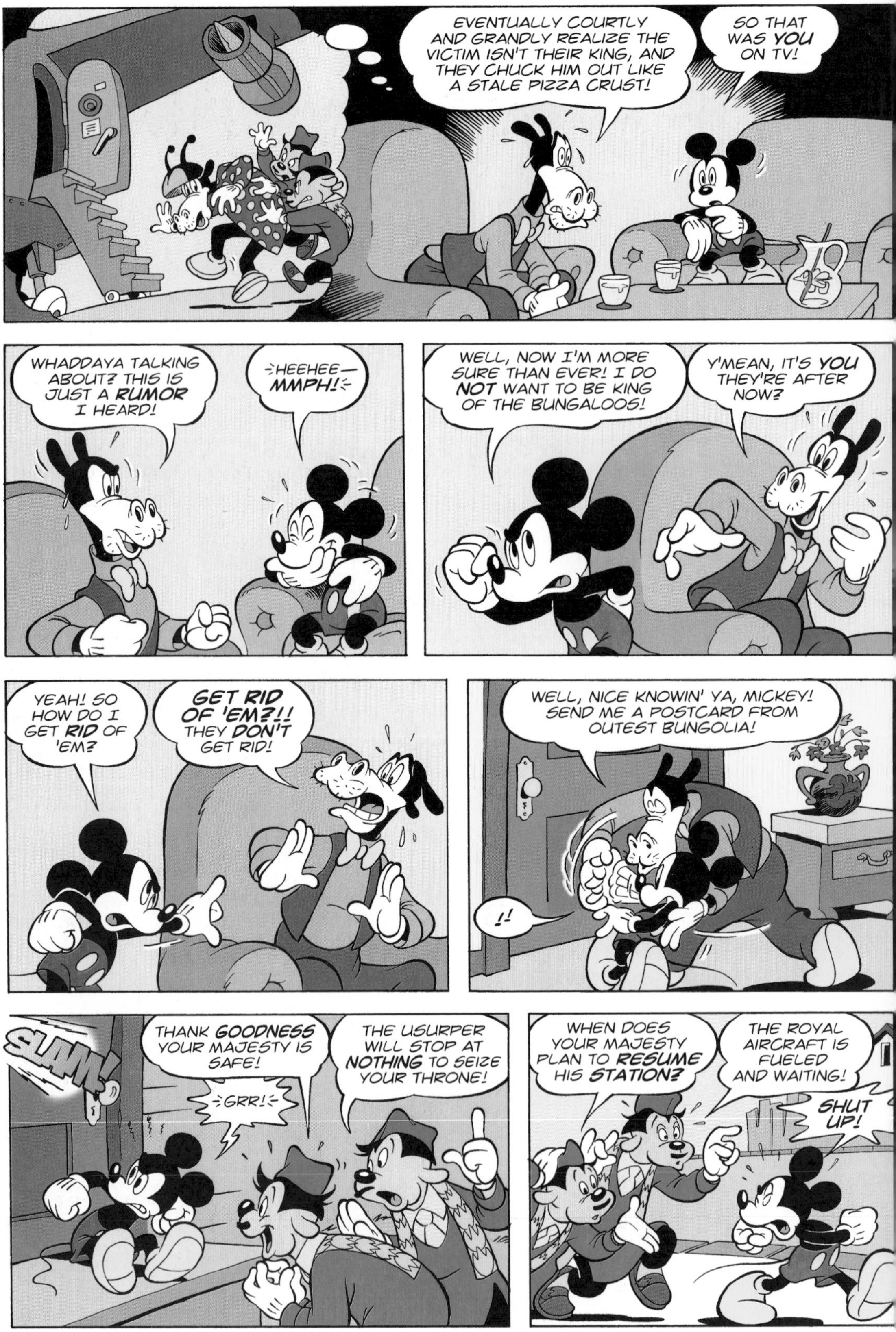

EVENTUALLY COURTLY AND GRANDLY REALIZE THE VICTIM ISN'T THEIR KING, AND THEY CHUCK HIM OUT LIKE A STALE PIZZA CRUST!
SO THAT WAS YOU ON TV!
WHADDAYA TALKING ABOUT? THIS IS JUST A RUMOR I HEARD!
HEEHEE— MMPH!
WELL, NOW I'M MORE SURE THAN EVER! I DO NOT WANT TO BE KING OF THE BUNGALOOS!
Y'MEAN, IT'S YOU THEY'RE AFTER NOW?
YEAH! SO HOW DO I GET RID OF 'EM?
GET RID OF 'EM?!! THEY DON'T GET RID!
WELL, NICE KNOWIN' YA, MICKEY! SEND ME A POSTCARD FROM OUTEST BUNGOLIA!
!!
SLAM!
THANK GOODNESS YOUR MAJESTY IS SAFE!
GRR!
THE USURPER WILL STOP AT NOTHING TO SEIZE YOUR THRONE!
WHEN DOES YOUR MAJESTY PLAN TO RESUME HIS STATION?
THE ROYAL AIRCRAFT IS FUELED AND WAITING!
SHUT UP!

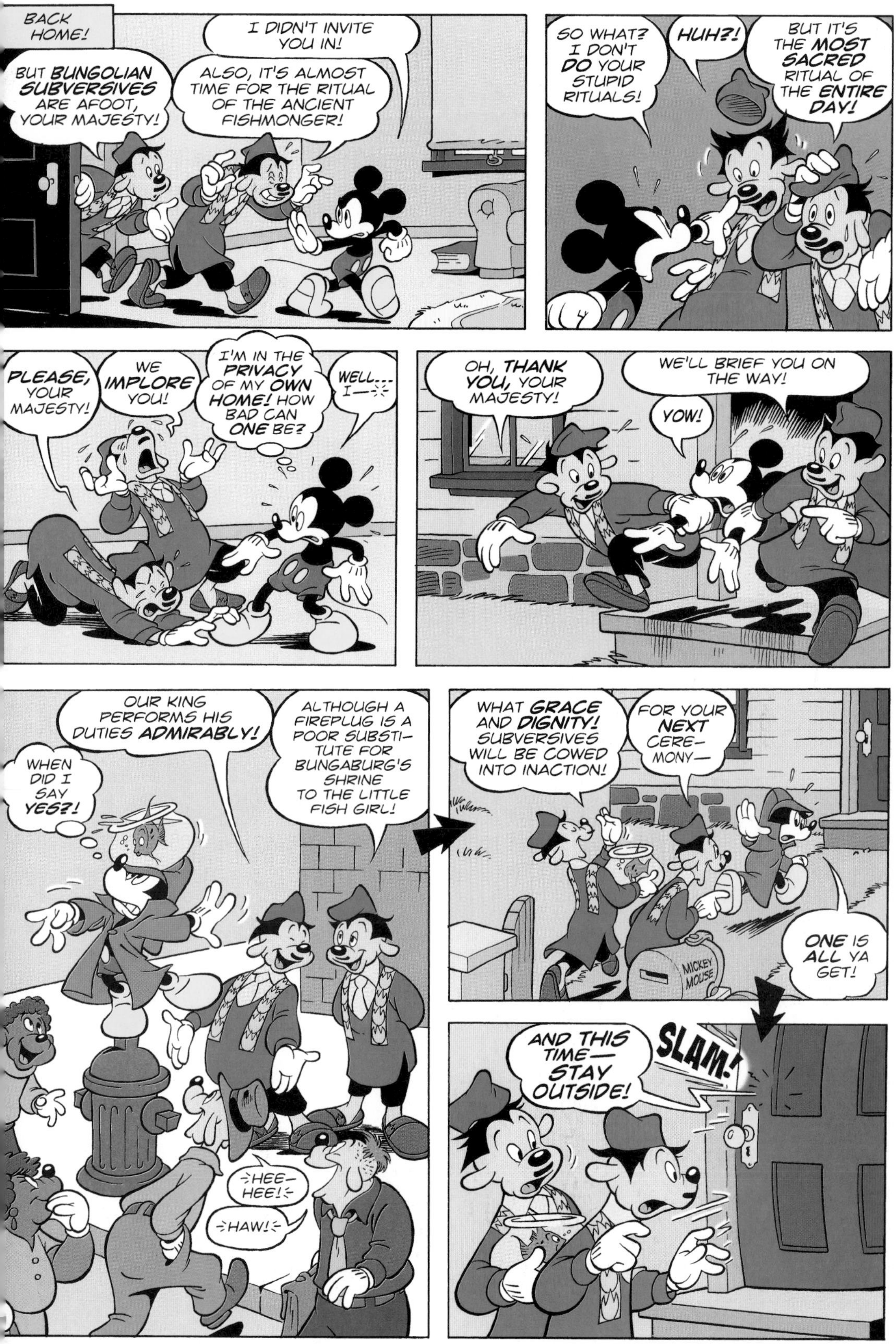
BACK HOME!
BUT BUNGOLIAN SUBVERSIVES ARE AFOOT, YOUR MAJESTY!
I DIDN'T INVITE YOU IN!
ALSO, IT'S ALMOST TIME FOR THE RITUAL OF THE ANCIENT FISHMONGER!
SO WHAT? I DON'T DO YOUR STUPID RITUALS!
HUH?!
BUT IT'S THE MOST SACRED RITUAL OF THE ENTIRE DAY!
PLEASE, YOUR MAJESTY!
WE IMPLORE YOU!
I'M IN THE PRIVACY OF MY OWN HOME! HOW BAD CAN ONE BE?
WELL... I—
OH, THANK YOU, YOUR MAJESTY!
WE'LL BRIEF YOU ON THE WAY!
YOW!
OUR KING PERFORMS HIS DUTIES ADMIRABLY!
WHEN DID I SAY YES?!
ALTHOUGH A FIREPLUG IS A POOR SUBSTI-TUTE FOR BUNGABURG'S SHRINE TO THE LITTLE FISH GIRL!
HEE-HEE!
HAW!
WHAT GRACE AND DIGNITY! SUBVERSIVES WILL BE COWED INTO INACTION!
FOR YOUR NEXT CERE-MONY—
ONE IS ALL YA GET!
MICKEY MOUSE
AND THIS TIME— STAY OUTSIDE!
SLAM!

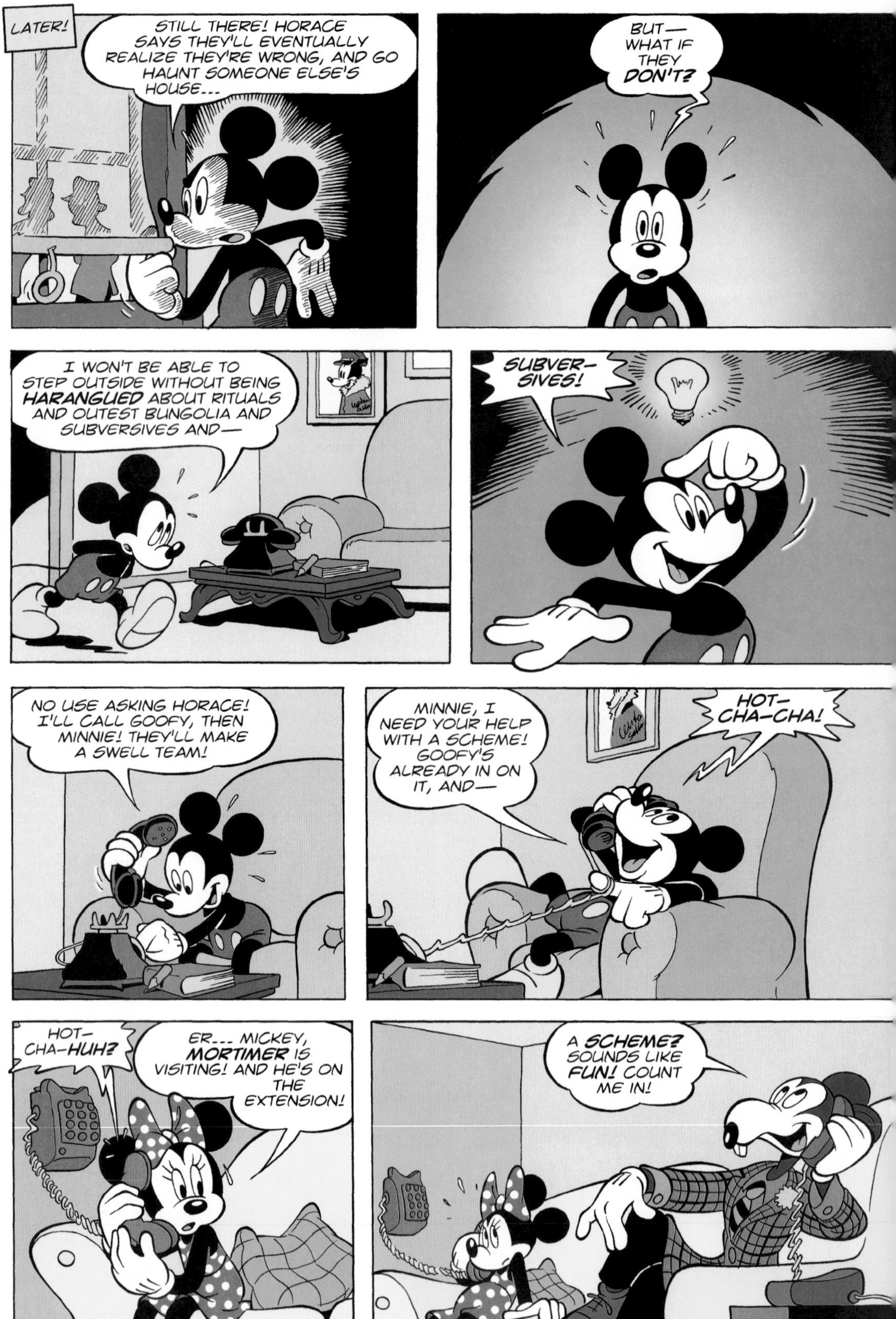
LATER!
STILL THERE! HORACE SAYS THEY'LL EVENTUALLY REALIZE THEY'RE WRONG, AND GO HAUNT SOMEONE ELSE'S HOUSE...
BUT— WHAT IF THEY DON'T?
I WON'T BE ABLE TO STEP OUTSIDE WITHOUT BEING HARANGUED ABOUT RITUALS AND OUTEST BUNGOLIA AND SUBVERSIVES AND—
SUBVER-SIVES!
NO USE ASKING HORACE! I'LL CALL GOOFY, THEN MINNIE! THEY'LL MAKE A SWELL TEAM!
MINNIE, I NEED YOUR HELP WITH A SCHEME! GOOFY'S ALREADY IN ON IT, AND—
HOT-CHA-CHA!
HOT-CHA-HUH?
ER... MICKEY, MORTIMER IS VISITING! AND HE'S ON THE EXTENSION!
A SCHEME? SOUNDS LIKE FUN! COUNT ME IN!

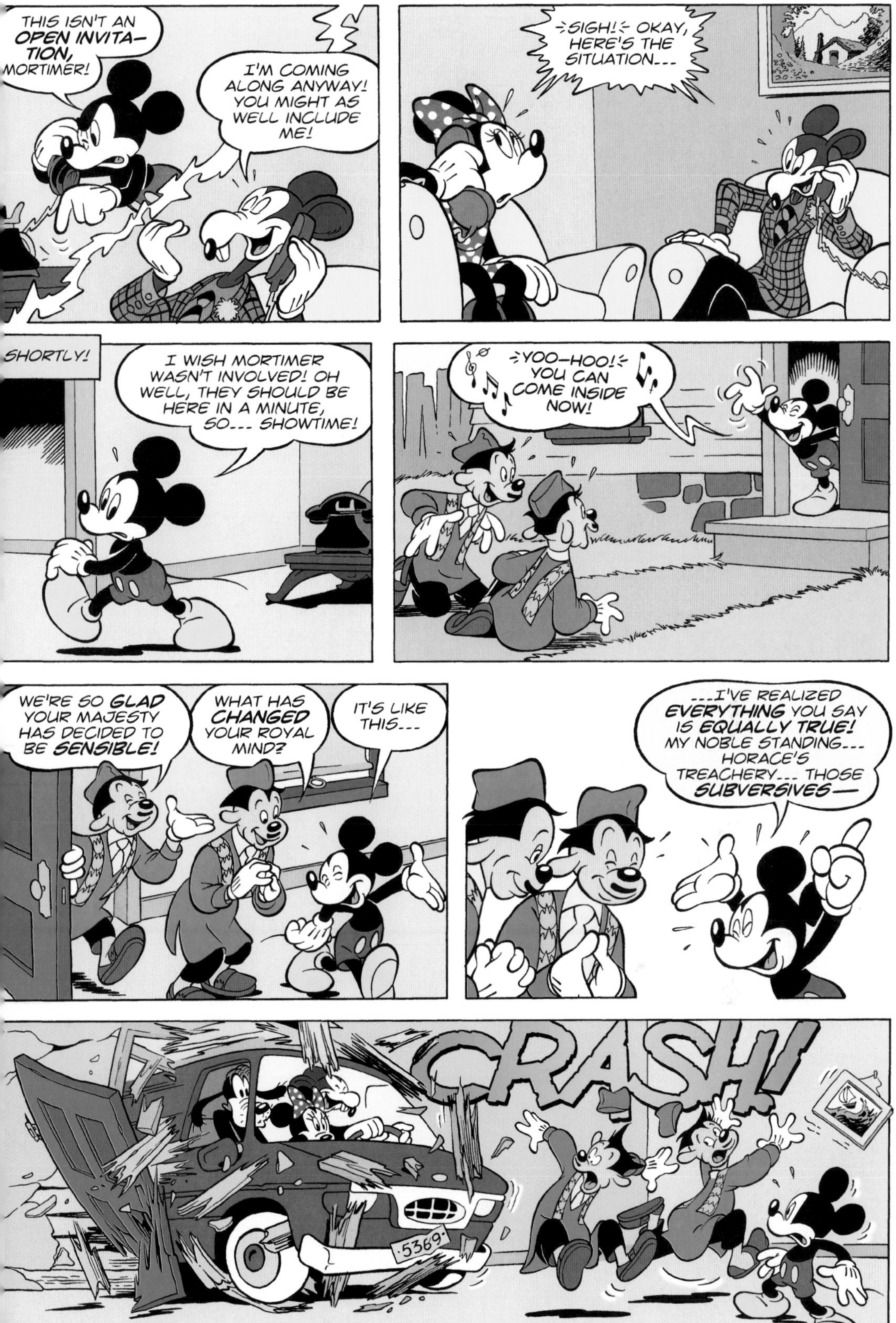
THIS ISN'T AN OPEN INVITATION, MORTIMER!
I'M COMING ALONG ANYWAY! YOU MIGHT AS WELL INCLUDE ME!
-SIGH!- OKAY, HERE'S THE SITUATION...
SHORTLY!
I WISH MORTIMER WASN'T INVOLVED! OH WELL, THEY SHOULD BE HERE IN A MINUTE, SO... SHOWTIME!
-YOO-HOO!- YOU CAN COME INSIDE NOW!
WE'RE SO GLAD YOUR MAJESTY HAS DECIDED TO BE SENSIBLE!
WHAT HAS CHANGED YOUR ROYAL MIND?
IT'S LIKE THIS...
...I'VE REALIZED EVERYTHING YOU SAY IS EQUALLY TRUE! MY NOBLE STANDING... HORACE'S TREACHERY... THOSE SUBVERSIVES—
CRASH!
5369

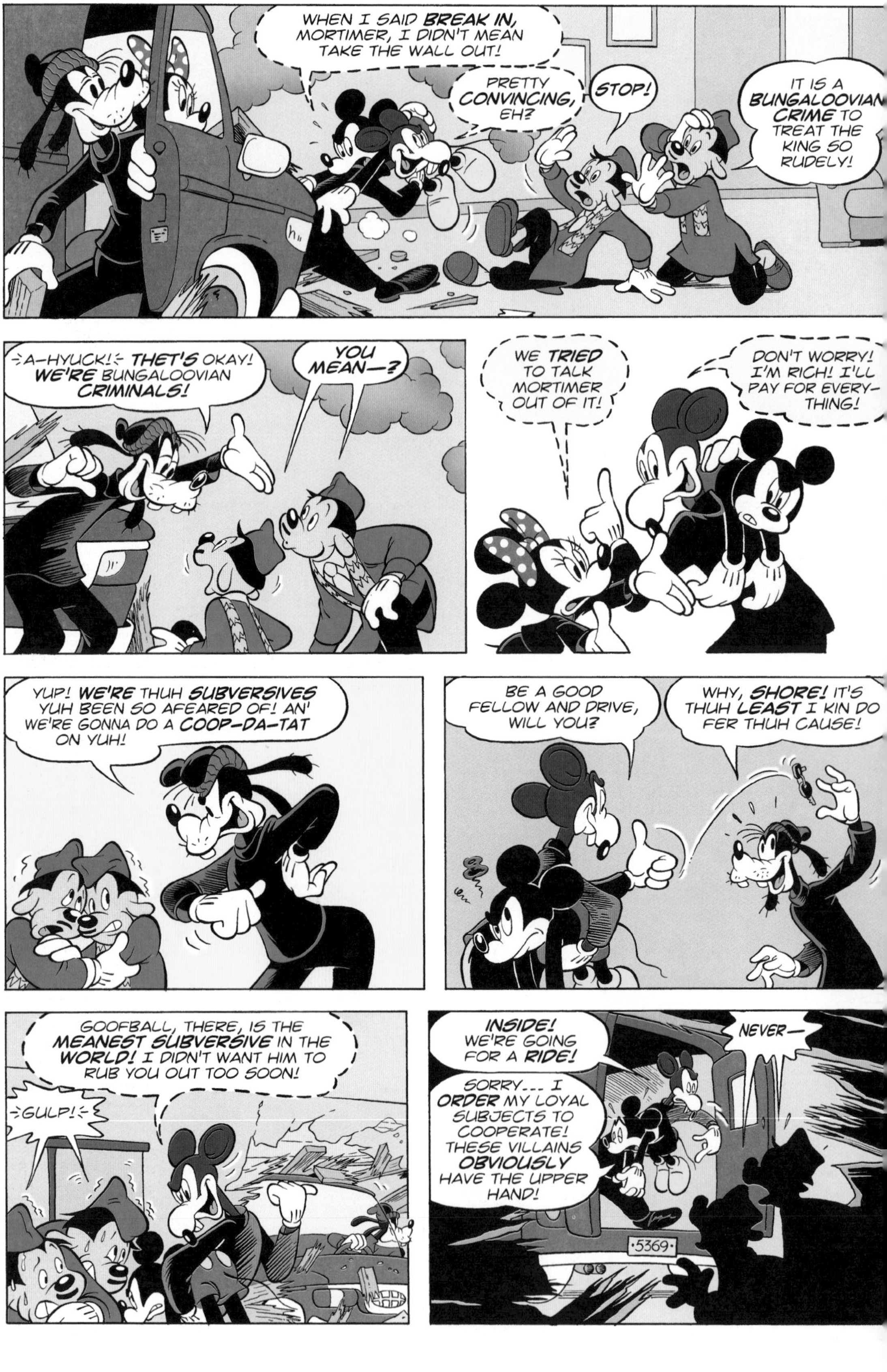
WHEN I SAID **BREAK IN,** MORTIMER, I DIDN'T MEAN TAKE THE WALL OUT!
PRETTY **CONVINCING,** EH?
STOP!
IT IS A **BUNGALOOVIAN CRIME** TO TREAT THE KING SO RUDELY!
A-HYUCK! **THET'S** OKAY! **WE'RE** BUNGALOOVIAN **CRIMINALS!**
YOU MEAN—?
WE **TRIED** TO TALK MORTIMER OUT OF IT!
DON'T WORRY! I'M RICH! I'LL PAY FOR EVERYTHING!
YUP! **WE'RE** THUH **SUBVERSIVES** YUH BEEN SO AFEARED OF! AN' WE'RE GONNA DO A **COOP-DA-TAT** ON YUH!
BE A GOOD FELLOW AND DRIVE, WILL YOU?
WHY, **SHORE!** IT'S THUH **LEAST** I KIN DO FER THUH CAUSE!
GOOFBALL, THERE, IS THE **MEANEST SUBVERSIVE** IN THE **WORLD!** I DIDN'T WANT HIM TO RUB YOU OUT TOO SOON!
GULP!
INSIDE! WE'RE GOING FOR A **RIDE!**
SORRY... I **ORDER** MY LOYAL SUBJECTS TO COOPERATE! THESE VILLAINS **OBVIOUSLY** HAVE THE UPPER HAND!
NEVER—
5369

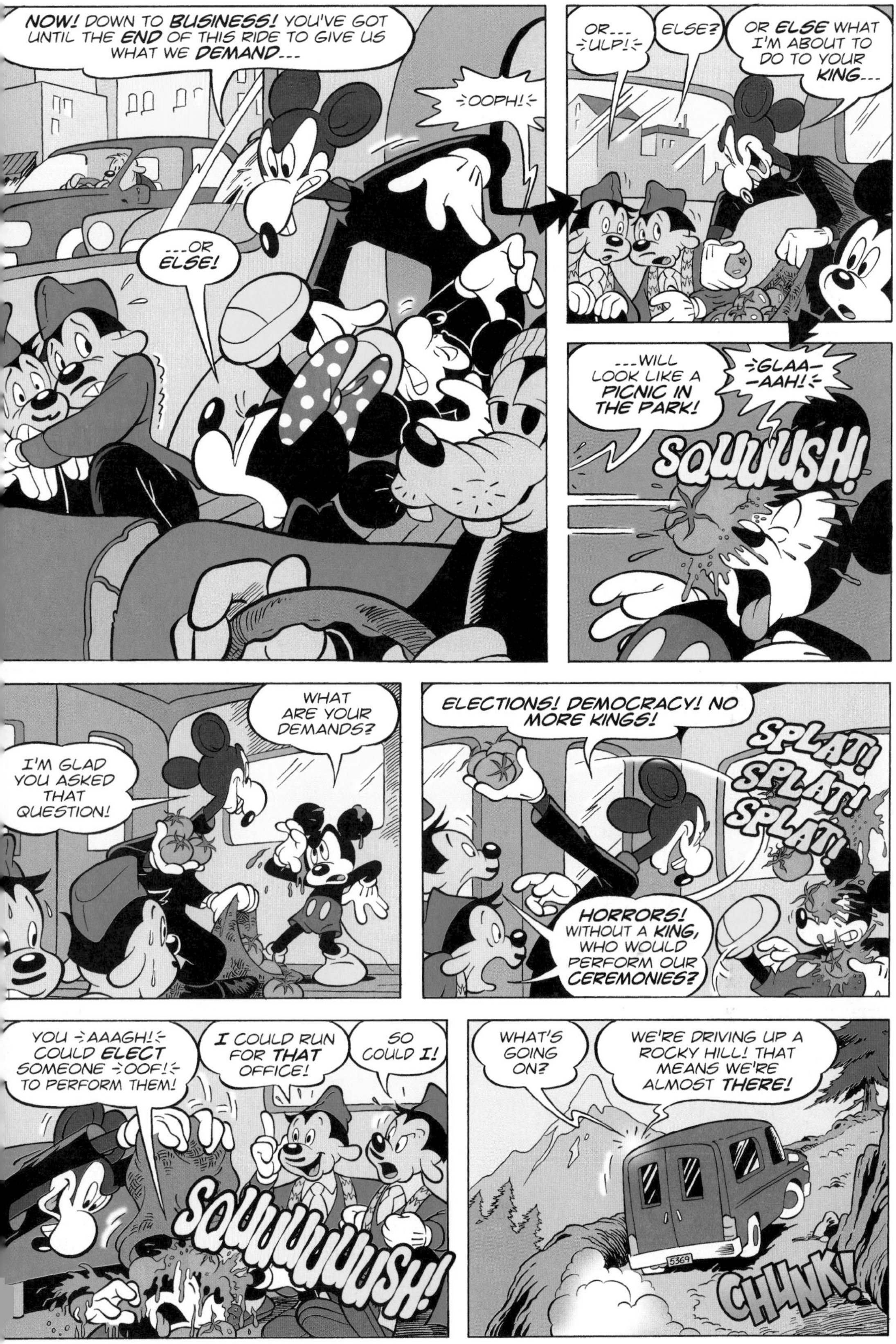
NOW! DOWN TO BUSINESS! YOU'VE GOT UNTIL THE END OF THIS RIDE TO GIVE US WHAT WE DEMAND---
-OOPH!-
---OR ELSE!
OR--- -ULP!-
ELSE?
OR ELSE WHAT I'M ABOUT TO DO TO YOUR KING---
---WILL LOOK LIKE A PICNIC IN THE PARK!
-GLAA--AAH!-
SQUUUSH!
I'M GLAD YOU ASKED THAT QUESTION!
WHAT ARE YOUR DEMANDS?
ELECTIONS! DEMOCRACY! NO MORE KINGS!
SPLAT! SPLAT! SPLAT!
HORRORS! WITHOUT A KING, WHO WOULD PERFORM OUR CEREMONIES?
YOU -AAAGH!- COULD ELECT SOMEONE -OOF!- TO PERFORM THEM!
I COULD RUN FOR THAT OFFICE!
SO COULD I!
SQUUUUUUUSH!
WHAT'S GOING ON?
WE'RE DRIVING UP A ROCKY HILL! THAT MEANS WE'RE ALMOST THERE!
5369
CHUNK!

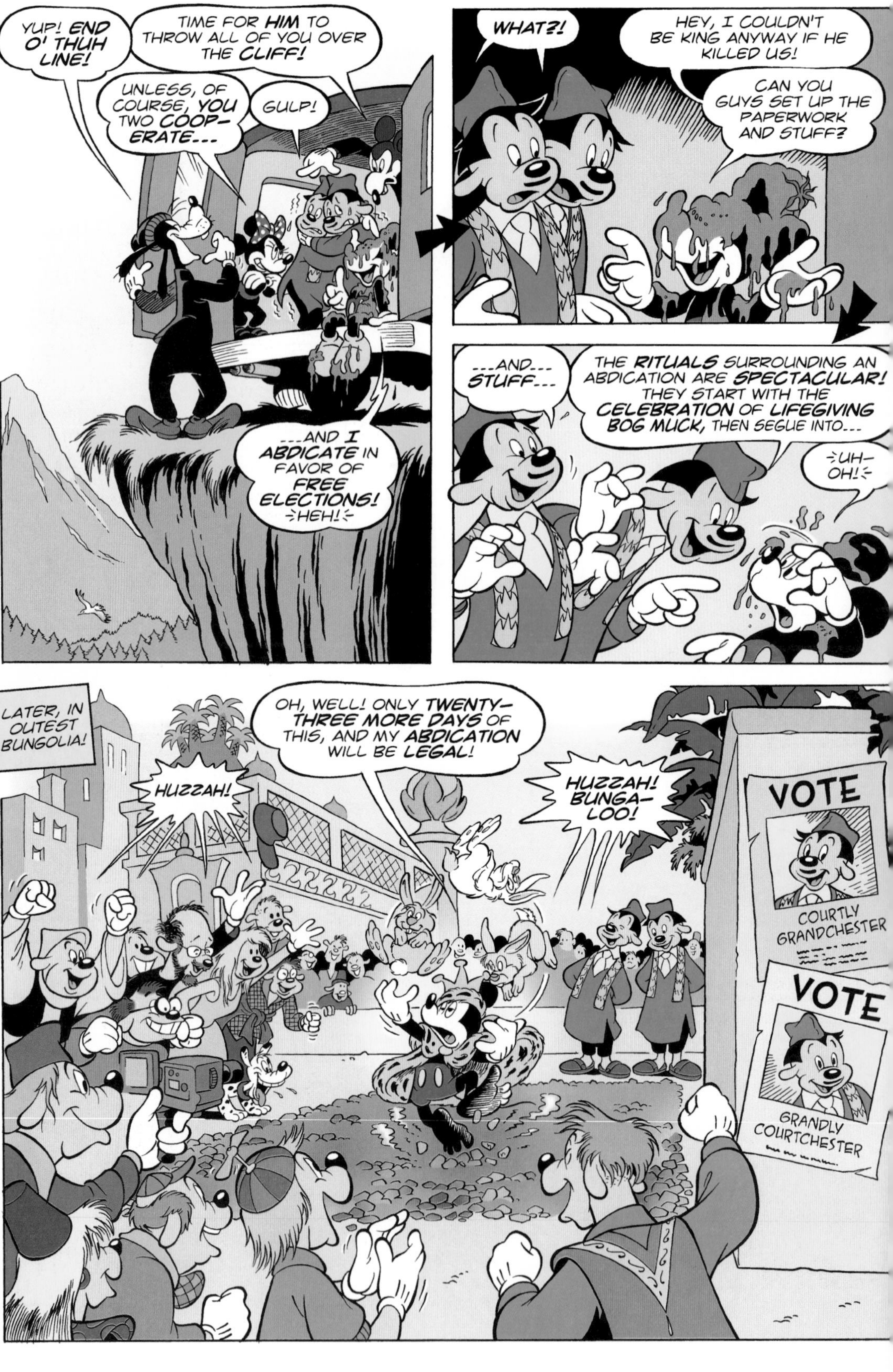

YUP! END O' THUH LINE!
TIME FOR HIM TO THROW ALL OF YOU OVER THE CLIFF!
UNLESS, OF COURSE, YOU TWO COOP-ERATE...
GULP!
...AND I ABDICATE IN FAVOR OF FREE ELECTIONS! -HEH!-
WHAT?!
HEY, I COULDN'T BE KING ANYWAY IF HE KILLED US!
CAN YOU GUYS SET UP THE PAPERWORK AND STUFF?
...AND... STUFF...
THE RITUALS SURROUNDING AN ABDICATION ARE SPECTACULAR! THEY START WITH THE CELEBRATION OF LIFEGIVING BOG MUCK, THEN SEGUE INTO...
-UH-OH!-
LATER, IN OUTEST BUNGOLIA!
OH, WELL! ONLY TWENTY-THREE MORE DAYS OF THIS, AND MY ABDICATION WILL BE LEGAL!
HUZZAH!
HUZZAH! BUNGA-LOO!
VOTE
COURTLY GRANDCHESTER
VOTE
GRANDLY COURTCHESTER

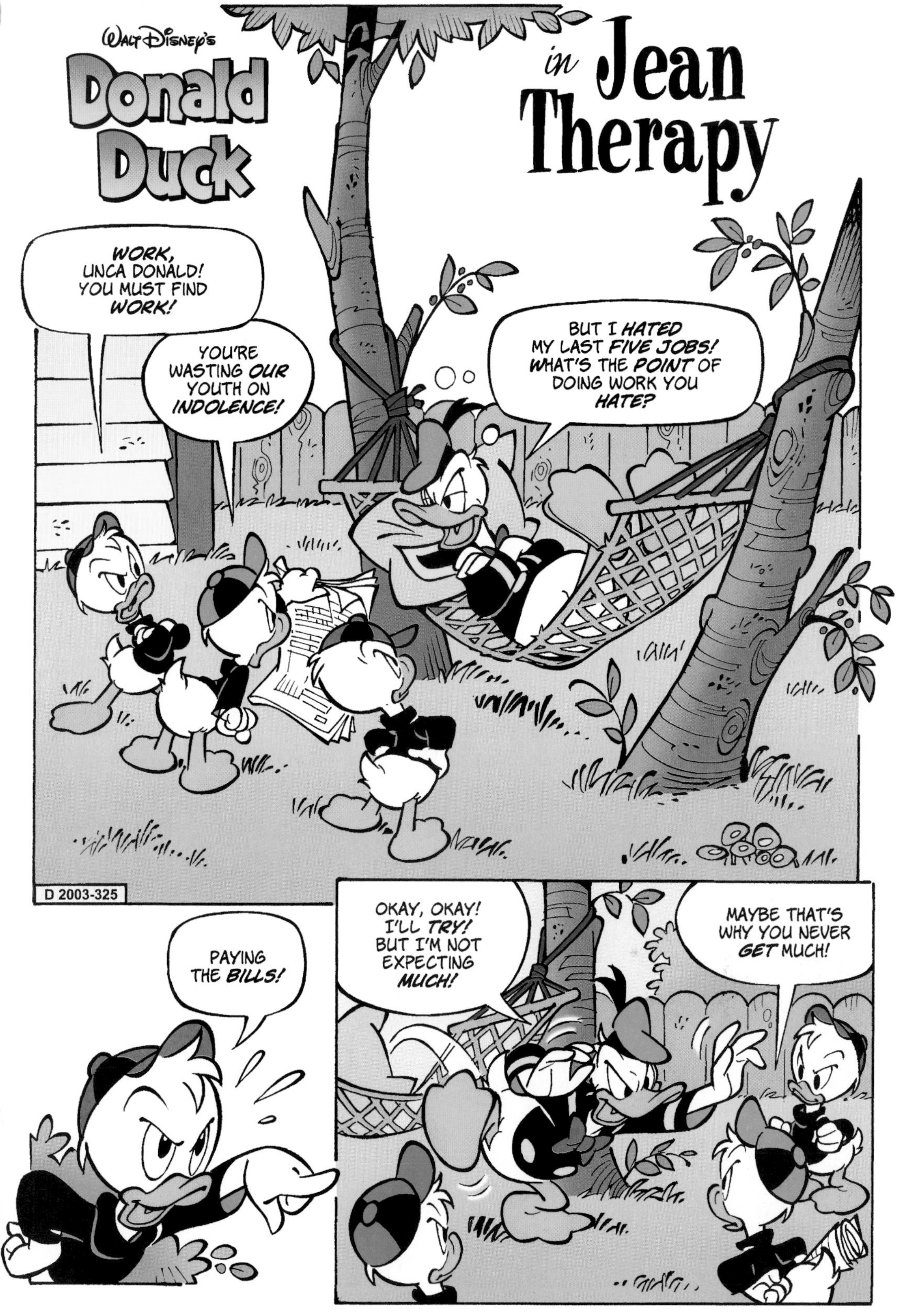

Walt Disney's Donald Duck in Jean Therapy
WORK, UNCA DONALD! YOU MUST FIND WORK!
YOU'RE WASTING OUR YOUTH ON INDOLENCE!
BUT I HATED MY LAST FIVE JOBS! WHAT'S THE POINT OF DOING WORK YOU HATE?
D 2003-325
PAYING THE BILLS!
OKAY, OKAY! I'LL TRY! BUT I'M NOT EXPECTING MUCH!
MAYBE THAT'S WHY YOU NEVER GET MUCH!

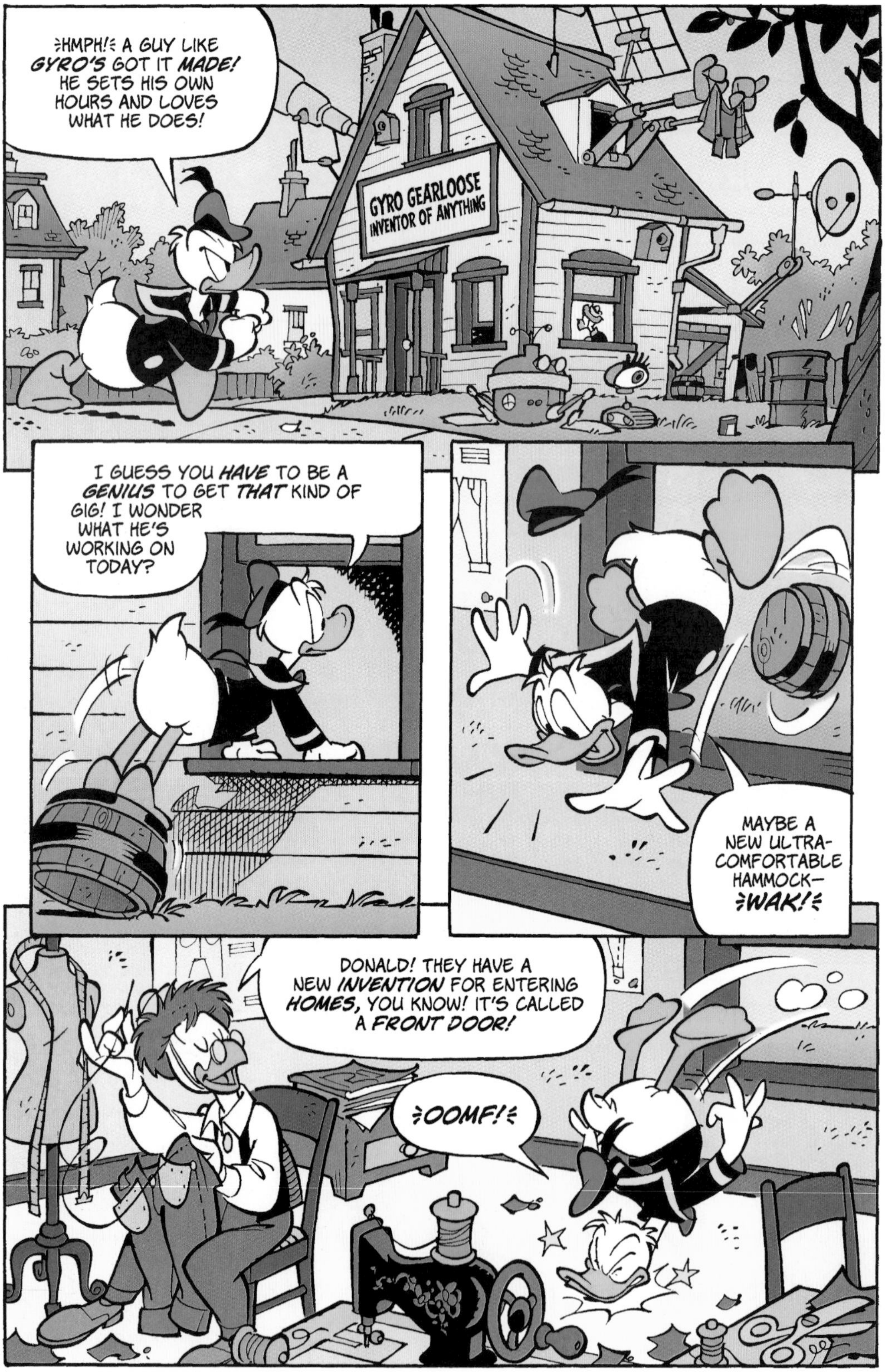

HMPH! A GUY LIKE GYRO'S GOT IT MADE! HE SETS HIS OWN HOURS AND LOVES WHAT HE DOES!
GYRO GEARLOOSE INVENTOR OF ANYTHING
I GUESS YOU HAVE TO BE A GENIUS TO GET THAT KIND OF GIG! I WONDER WHAT HE'S WORKING ON TODAY?
MAYBE A NEW ULTRA-COMFORTABLE HAMMOCK— WAK!
DONALD! THEY HAVE A NEW INVENTION FOR ENTERING HOMES, YOU KNOW! IT'S CALLED A FRONT DOOR!
OOMF!

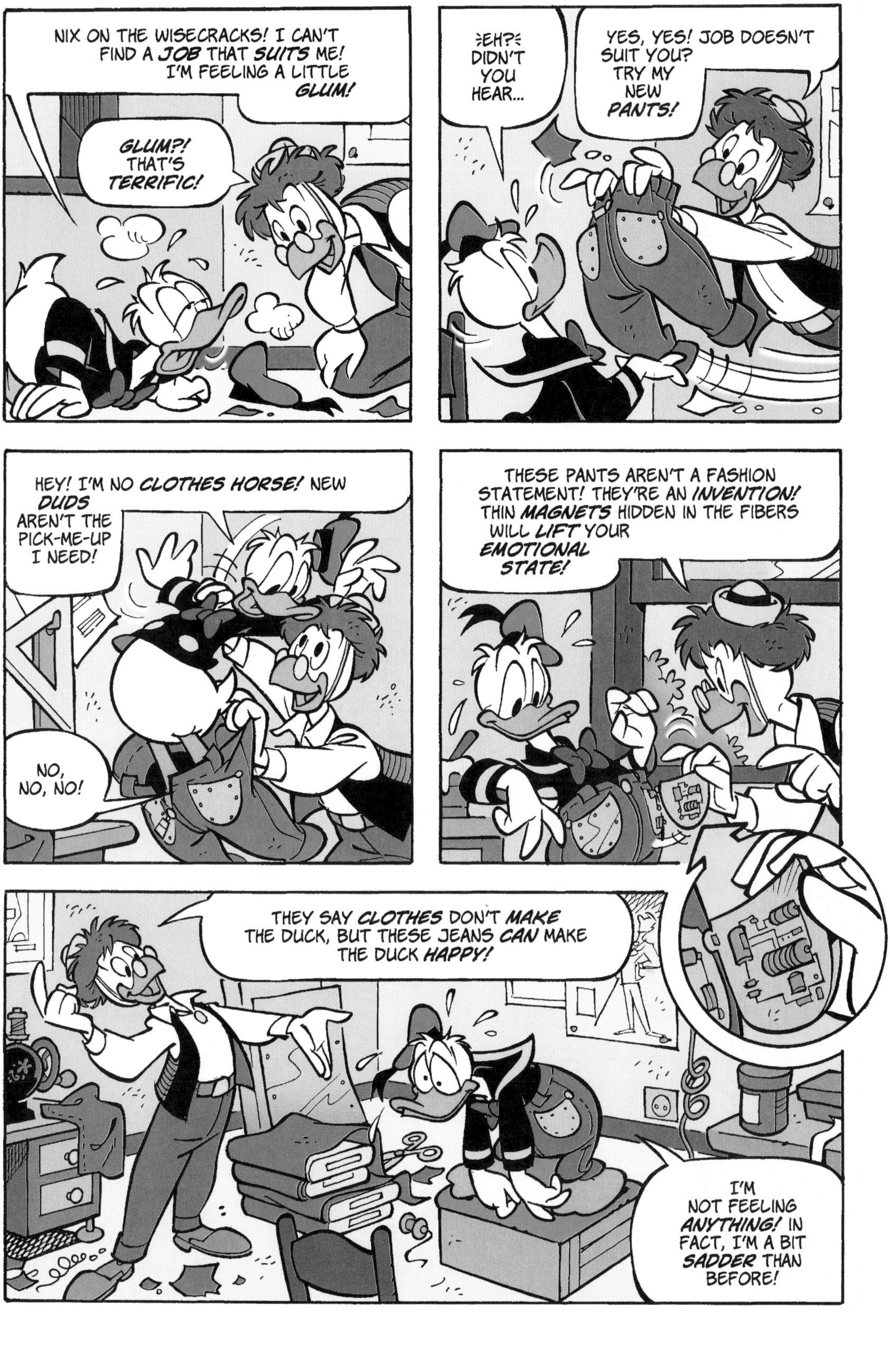

NIX ON THE WISECRACKS! I CAN'T FIND A JOB THAT SUITS ME! I'M FEELING A LITTLE GLUM!
GLUM?! THAT'S TERRIFIC!
EH?? DIDN'T YOU HEAR...
YES, YES! JOB DOESN'T SUIT YOU? TRY MY NEW PANTS!
HEY! I'M NO CLOTHES HORSE! NEW DUDS AREN'T THE PICK-ME-UP I NEED!
NO, NO, NO!
THESE PANTS AREN'T A FASHION STATEMENT! THEY'RE AN INVENTION! THIN MAGNETS HIDDEN IN THE FIBERS WILL LIFT YOUR EMOTIONAL STATE!
THEY SAY CLOTHES DON'T MAKE THE DUCK, BUT THESE JEANS CAN MAKE THE DUCK HAPPY!
I'M NOT FEELING ANYTHING! IN FACT, I'M A BIT SADDER THAN BEFORE!

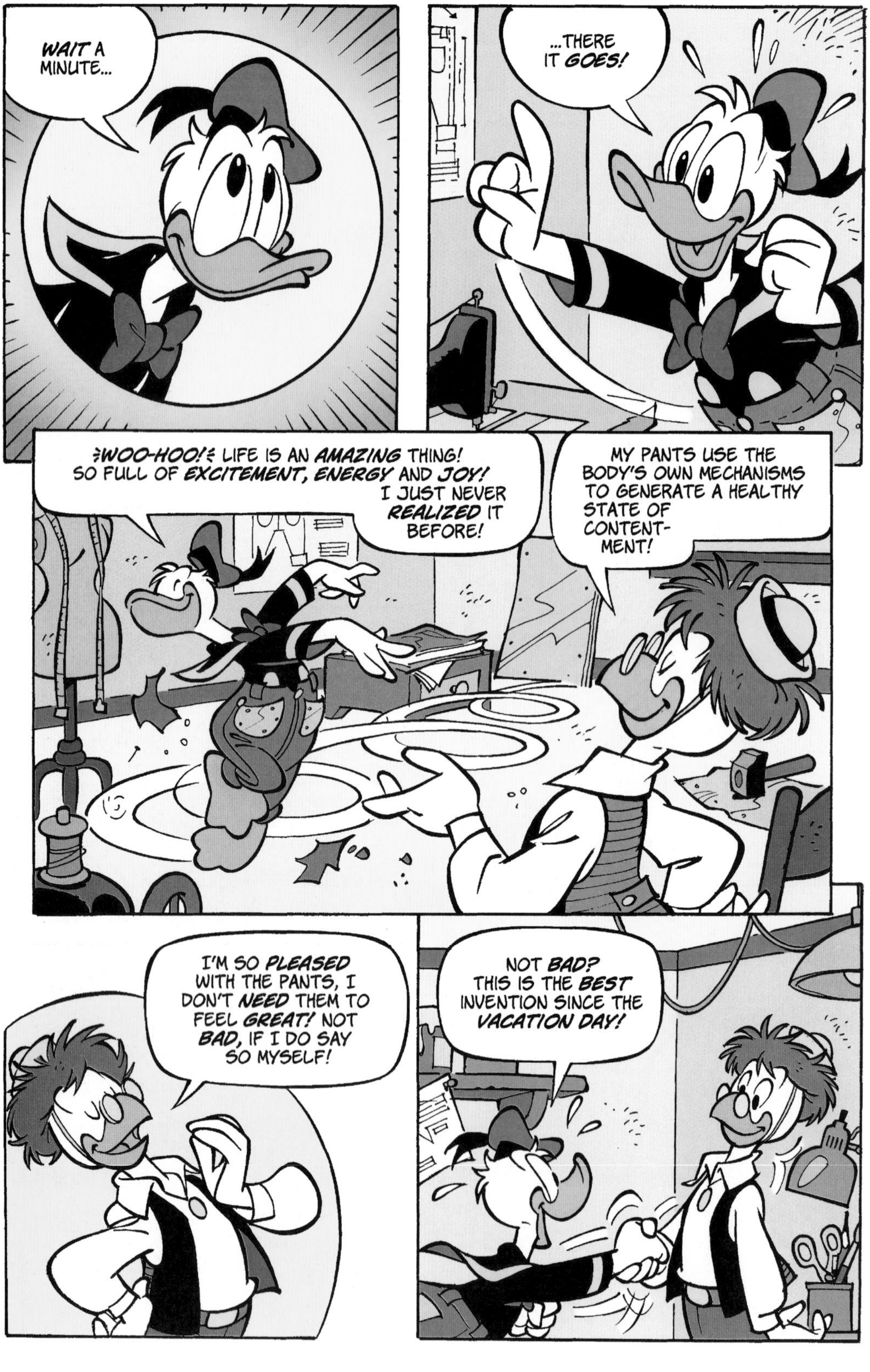
WAIT A MINUTE...
...THERE IT GOES!
WOO-HOO! LIFE IS AN AMAZING THING! SO FULL OF EXCITEMENT, ENERGY AND JOY! I JUST NEVER REALIZED IT BEFORE!
MY PANTS USE THE BODY'S OWN MECHANISMS TO GENERATE A HEALTHY STATE OF CONTENT- MENT!
I'M SO PLEASED WITH THE PANTS, I DON'T NEED THEM TO FEEL GREAT! NOT BAD, IF I DO SAY SO MYSELF!
NOT BAD? THIS IS THE BEST INVENTION SINCE THE VACATION DAY!

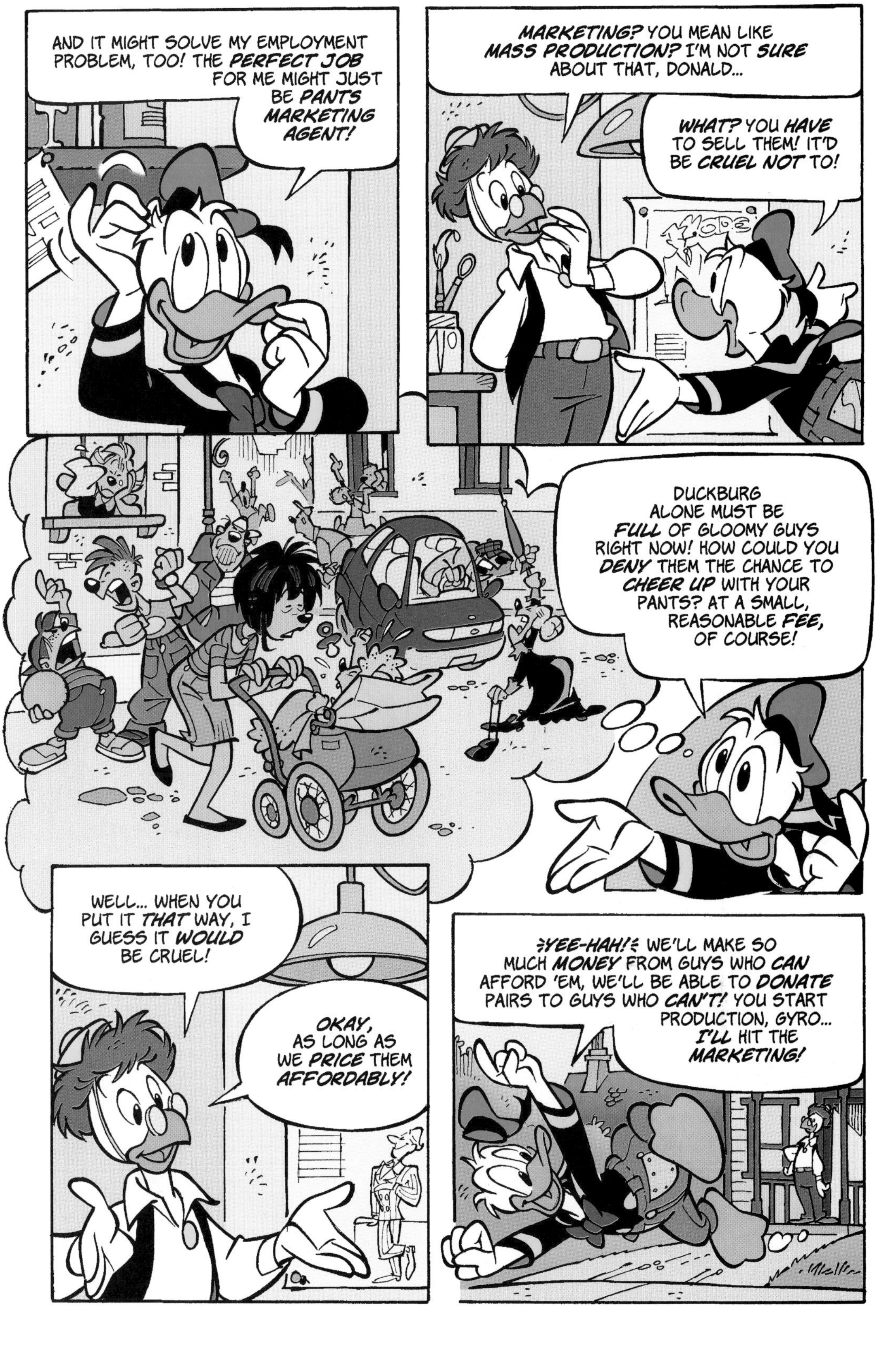
AND IT MIGHT SOLVE MY EMPLOYMENT PROBLEM, TOO! THE PERFECT JOB FOR ME MIGHT JUST BE PANTS MARKETING AGENT!
MARKETING? YOU MEAN LIKE MASS PRODUCTION? I'M NOT SURE ABOUT THAT, DONALD...
WHAT? YOU HAVE TO SELL THEM! IT'D BE CRUEL NOT TO!
DUCKBURG ALONE MUST BE FULL OF GLOOMY GUYS RIGHT NOW! HOW COULD YOU DENY THEM THE CHANCE TO CHEER UP WITH YOUR PANTS? AT A SMALL, REASONABLE FEE, OF COURSE!
WELL... WHEN YOU PUT IT THAT WAY, I GUESS IT WOULD BE CRUEL!
OKAY, AS LONG AS WE PRICE THEM AFFORDABLY!
YEE-HAH! WE'LL MAKE SO MUCH MONEY FROM GUYS WHO CAN AFFORD 'EM, WE'LL BE ABLE TO DONATE PAIRS TO GUYS WHO CAN'T! YOU START PRODUCTION, GYRO... I'LL HIT THE MARKETING!

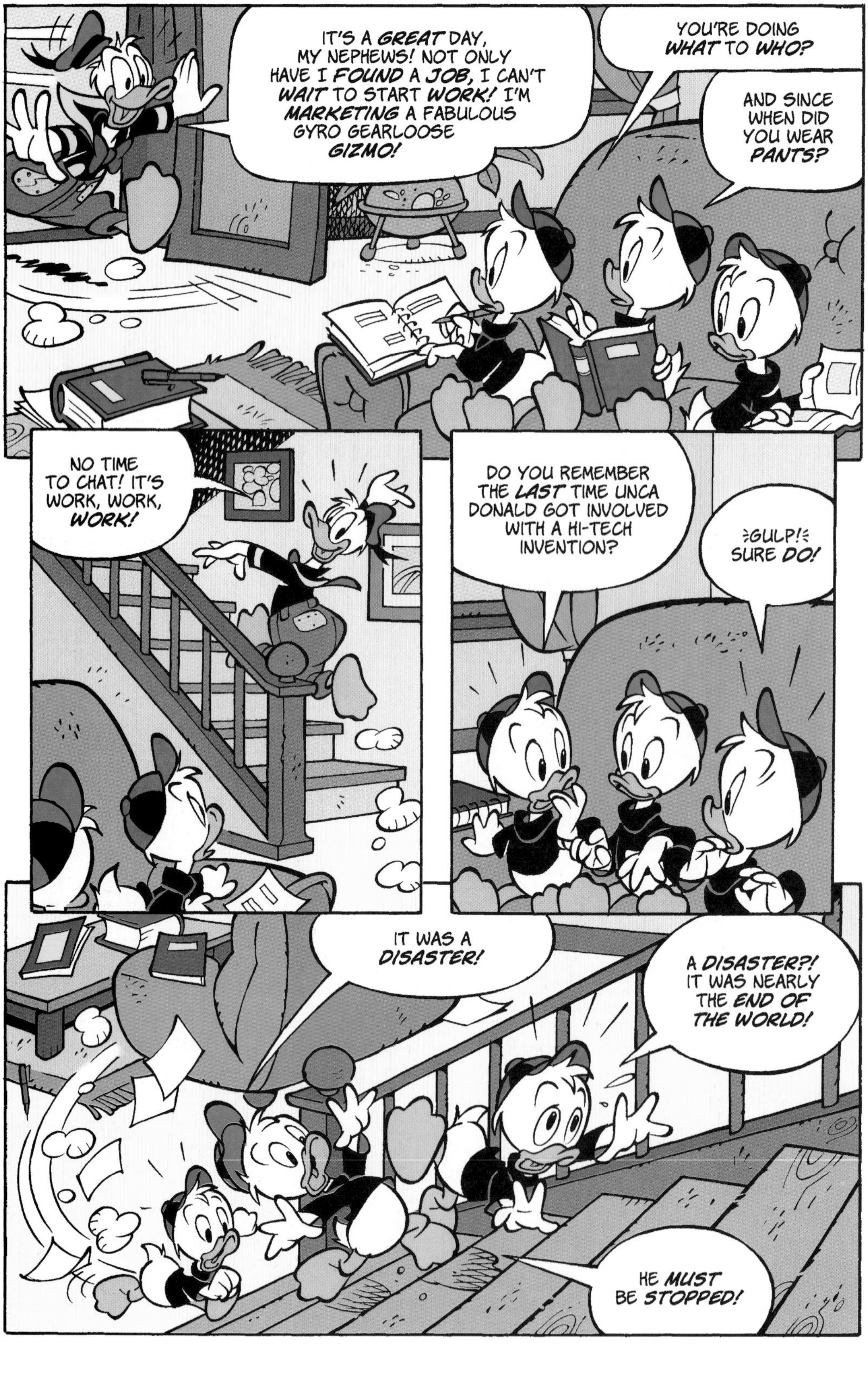
IT'S A GREAT DAY, MY NEPHEWS! NOT ONLY HAVE I FOUND A JOB, I CAN'T WAIT TO START WORK! I'M MARKETING A FABULOUS GYRO GEARLOOSE GIZMO!
YOU'RE DOING WHAT TO WHO?
AND SINCE WHEN DID YOU WEAR PANTS?
NO TIME TO CHAT! IT'S WORK, WORK, WORK!
DO YOU REMEMBER THE LAST TIME UNCA DONALD GOT INVOLVED WITH A HI-TECH INVENTION?
GULP! SURE DO!
IT WAS A DISASTER!
A DISASTER?! IT WAS NEARLY THE END OF THE WORLD!
HE MUST BE STOPPED!

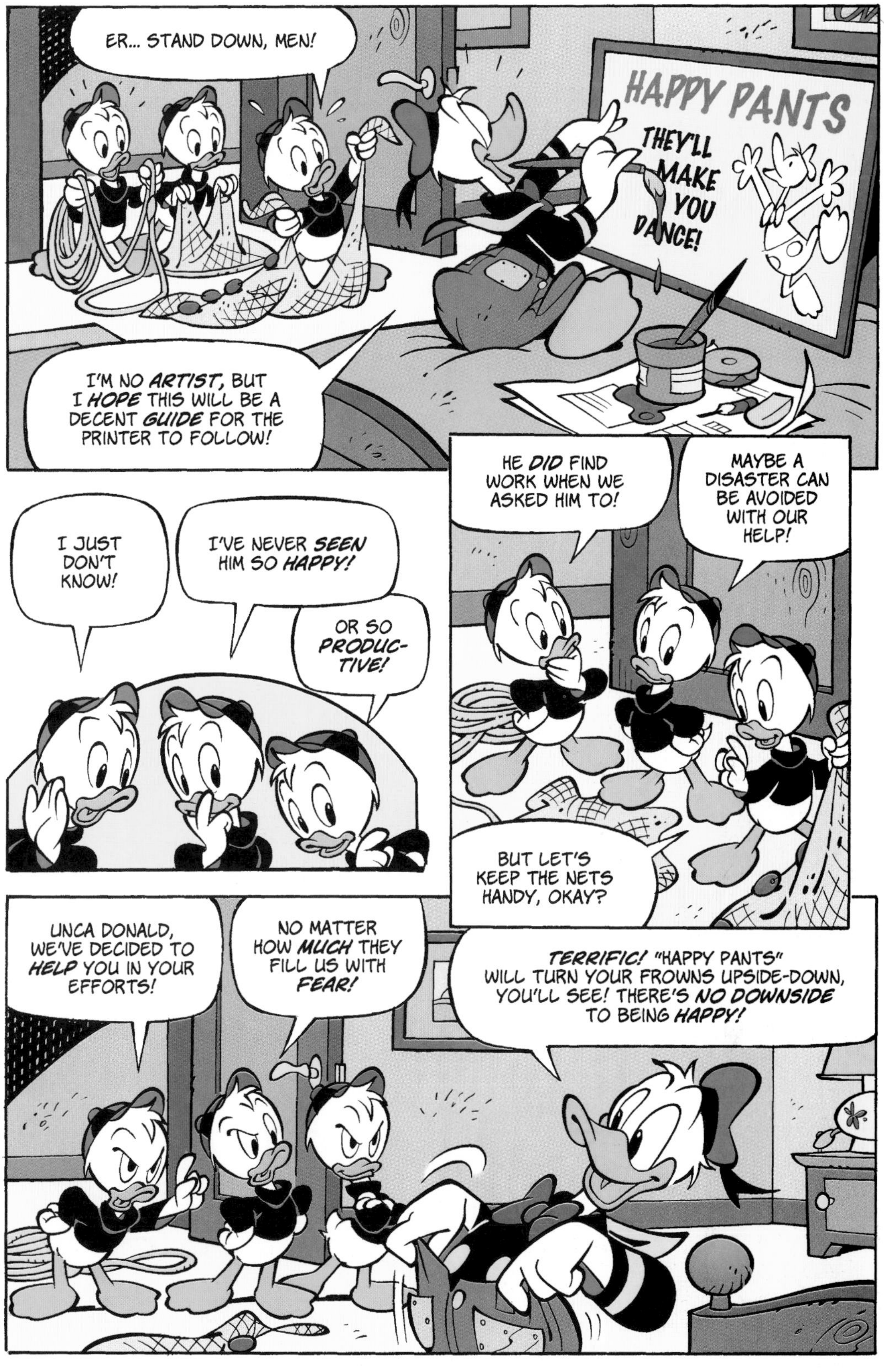
ER... STAND DOWN, MEN!
HAPPY PANTS
THEY'LL MAKE YOU DANCE!
I'M NO ARTIST, BUT I HOPE THIS WILL BE A DECENT GUIDE FOR THE PRINTER TO FOLLOW!
I JUST DON'T KNOW!
I'VE NEVER SEEN HIM SO HAPPY!
OR SO PRODUC-TIVE!
HE DID FIND WORK WHEN WE ASKED HIM TO!
MAYBE A DISASTER CAN BE AVOIDED WITH OUR HELP!
BUT LET'S KEEP THE NETS HANDY, OKAY?
UNCA DONALD, WE'VE DECIDED TO HELP YOU IN YOUR EFFORTS!
NO MATTER HOW MUCH THEY FILL US WITH FEAR!
TERRIFIC! "HAPPY PANTS" WILL TURN YOUR FROWNS UPSIDE-DOWN, YOU'LL SEE! THERE'S NO DOWNSIDE TO BEING HAPPY!

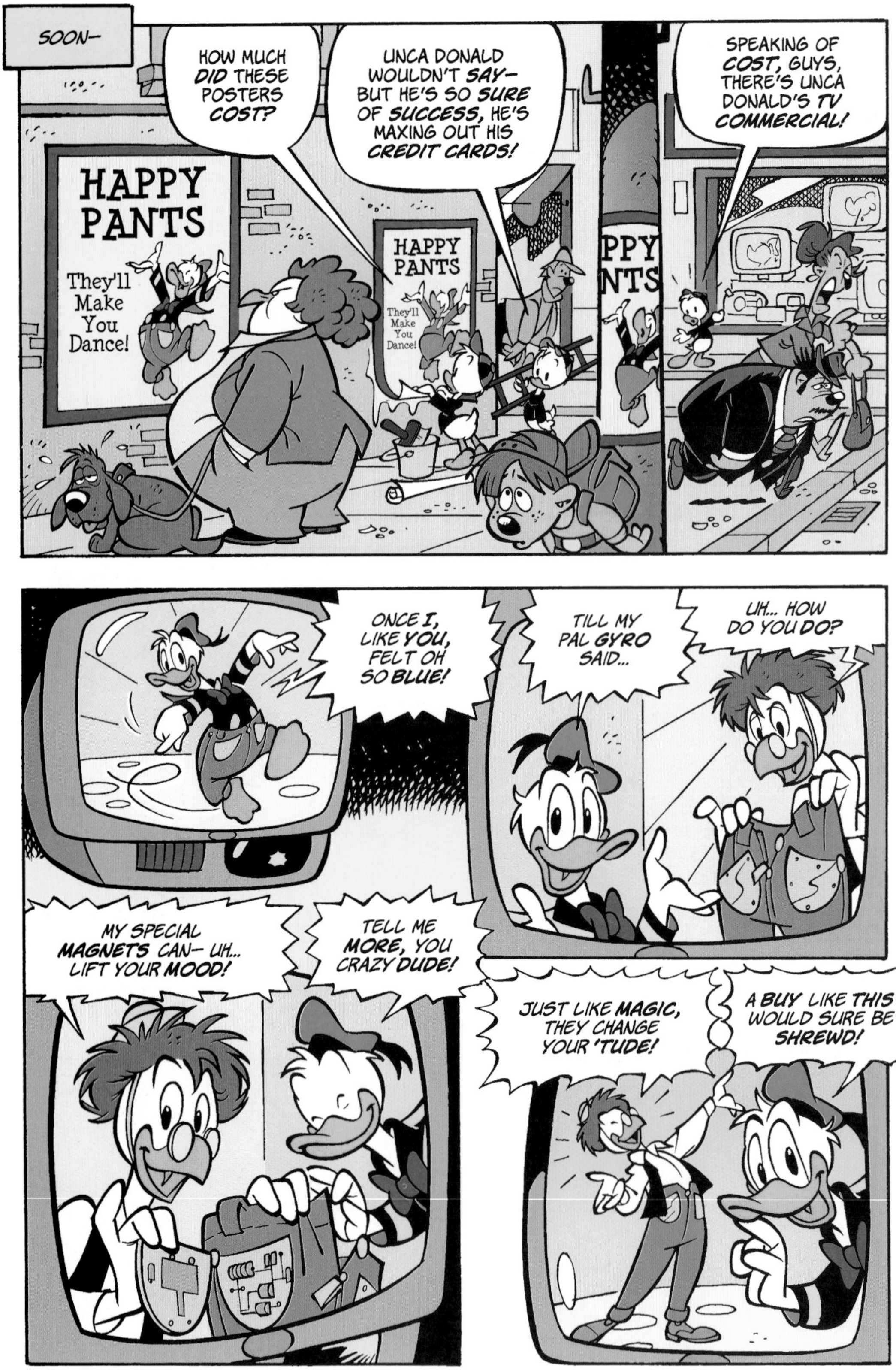
SOON—
HOW MUCH DID THESE POSTERS COST?
UNCA DONALD WOULDN'T SAY— BUT HE'S SO SURE OF SUCCESS, HE'S MAXING OUT HIS CREDIT CARDS!
SPEAKING OF COST, GUYS, THERE'S UNCA DONALD'S TV COMMERCIAL!
HAPPY PANTS They'll Make You Dance!
ONCE I, LIKE YOU, FELT OH SO BLUE!
TILL MY PAL GYRO SAID...
UH... HOW DO YOU DO?
MY SPECIAL MAGNETS CAN— UH... LIFT YOUR MOOD!
TELL ME MORE, YOU CRAZY DUDE!
JUST LIKE MAGIC, THEY CHANGE YOUR 'TUDE!
A BUY LIKE THIS WOULD SURE BE SHREWD!

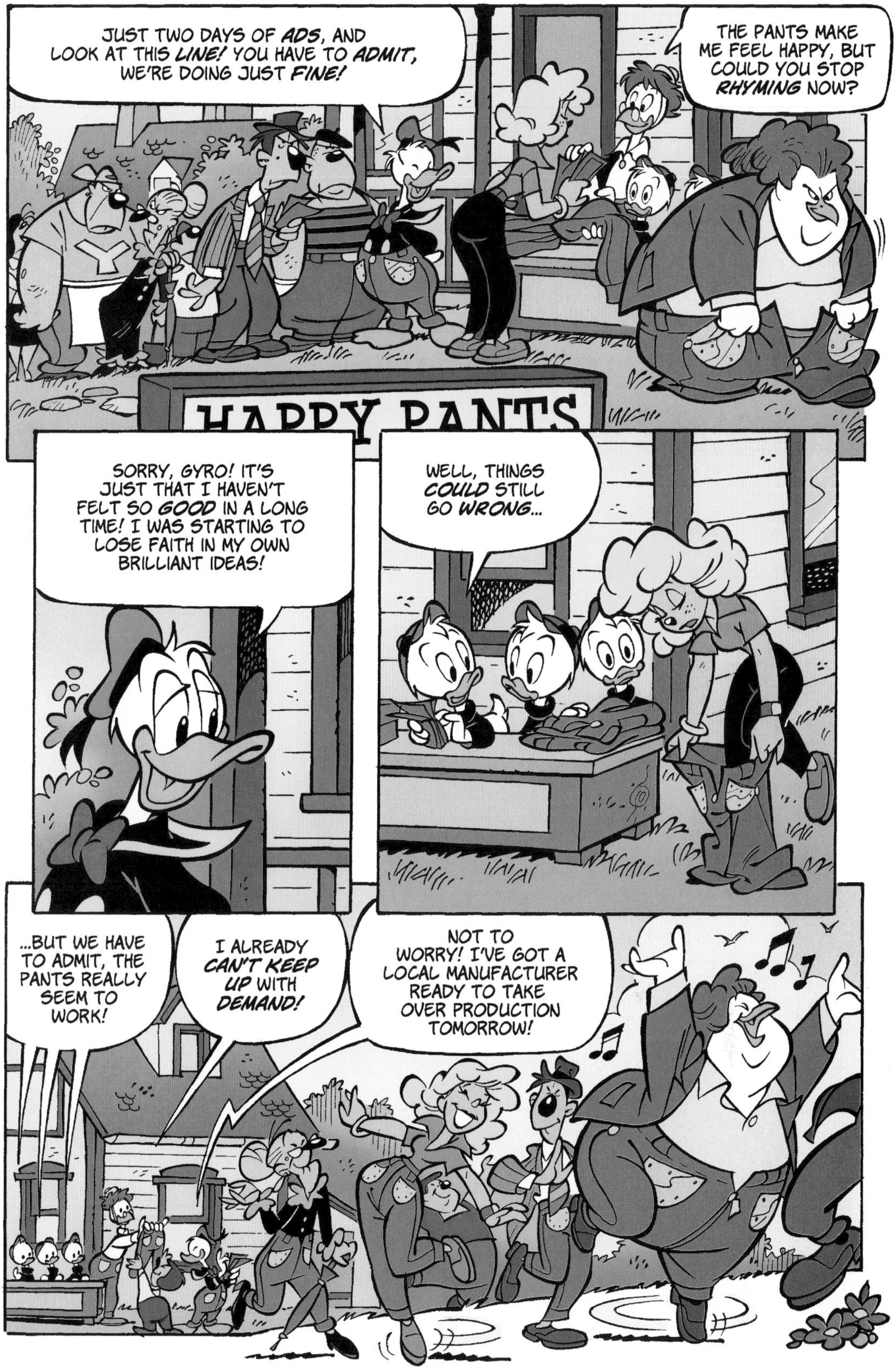
JUST TWO DAYS OF ADS, AND LOOK AT THIS LINE! YOU HAVE TO ADMIT, WE'RE DOING JUST FINE!
THE PANTS MAKE ME FEEL HAPPY, BUT COULD YOU STOP RHYMING NOW?
HAPPY PANTS
SORRY, GYRO! IT'S JUST THAT I HAVEN'T FELT SO GOOD IN A LONG TIME! I WAS STARTING TO LOSE FAITH IN MY OWN BRILLIANT IDEAS!
WELL, THINGS COULD STILL GO WRONG...
...BUT WE HAVE TO ADMIT, THE PANTS REALLY SEEM TO WORK!
I ALREADY CAN'T KEEP UP WITH DEMAND!
NOT TO WORRY! I'VE GOT A LOCAL MANUFACTURER READY TO TAKE OVER PRODUCTION TOMORROW!

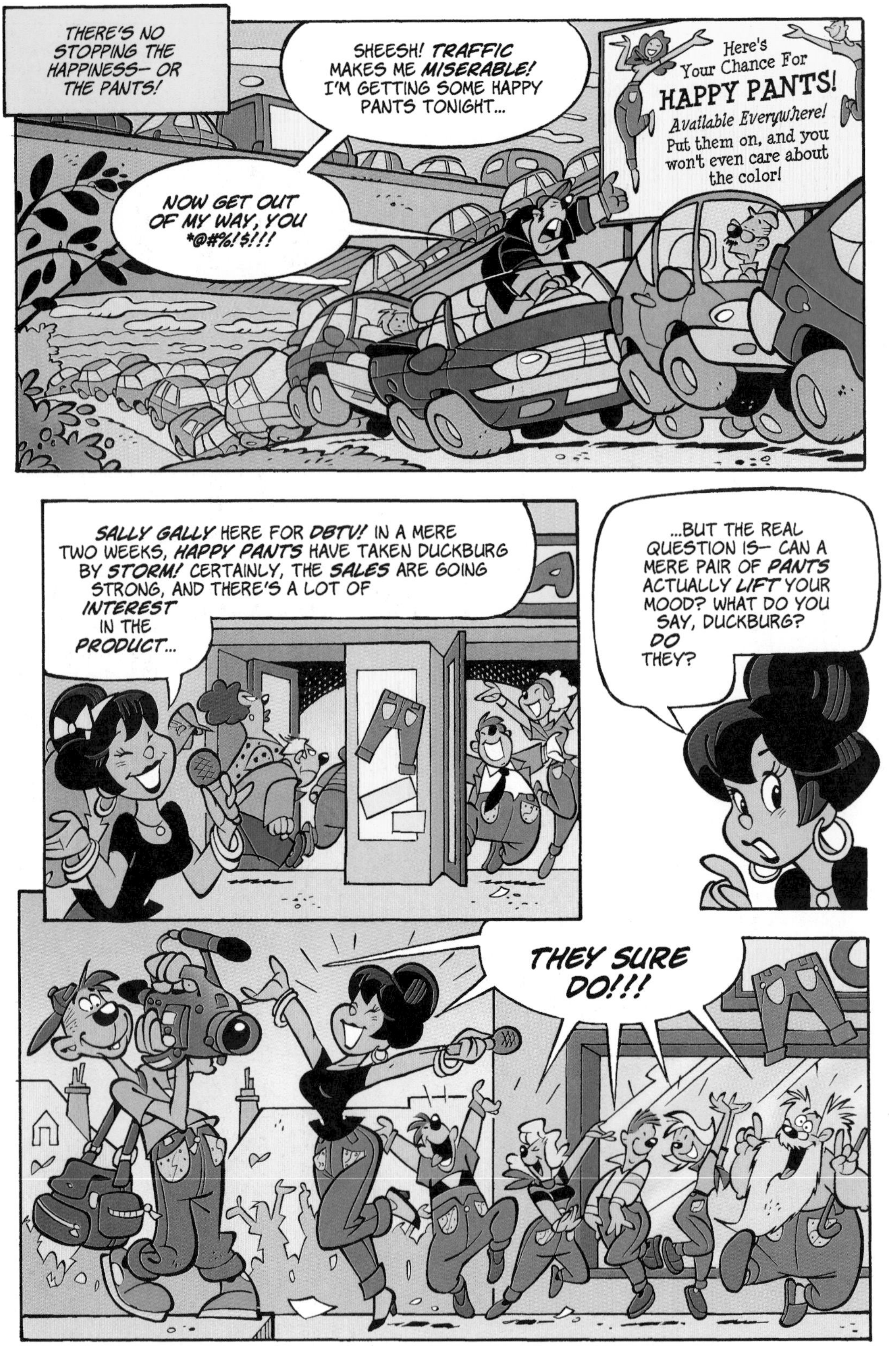
THERE'S NO STOPPING THE HAPPINESS— OR THE PANTS!
SHEESH! TRAFFIC MAKES ME MISERABLE! I'M GETTING SOME HAPPY PANTS TONIGHT...
NOW GET OUT OF MY WAY, YOU *@#%!$!!!
Here's Your Chance For HAPPY PANTS! Available Everywhere! Put them on, and you won't even care about the color!
SALLY GALLY HERE FOR DBTV! IN A MERE TWO WEEKS, HAPPY PANTS HAVE TAKEN DUCKBURG BY STORM! CERTAINLY, THE SALES ARE GOING STRONG, AND THERE'S A LOT OF INTEREST IN THE PRODUCT...
...BUT THE REAL QUESTION IS— CAN A MERE PAIR OF PANTS ACTUALLY LIFT YOUR MOOD? WHAT DO YOU SAY, DUCKBURG? DO THEY?
THEY SURE DO!!!

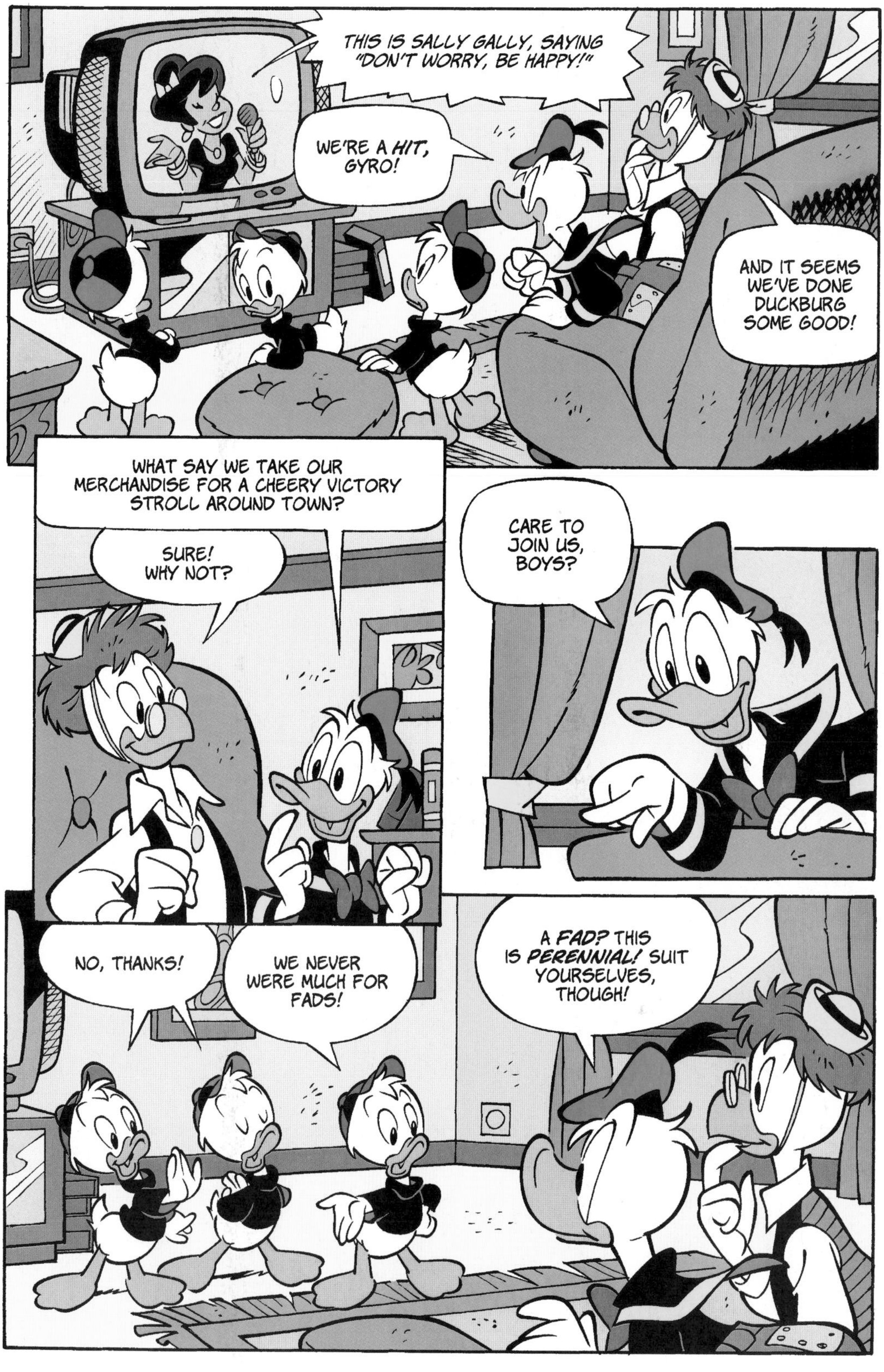
THIS IS SALLY GALLY, SAYING "DON'T WORRY, BE HAPPY!"
WE'RE A HIT, GYRO!
AND IT SEEMS WE'VE DONE DUCKBURG SOME GOOD!
WHAT SAY WE TAKE OUR MERCHANDISE FOR A CHEERY VICTORY STROLL AROUND TOWN?
SURE! WHY NOT?
CARE TO JOIN US, BOYS?
NO, THANKS!
WE NEVER WERE MUCH FOR FADS!
A FAD? THIS IS PERENNIAL! SUIT YOURSELVES, THOUGH!

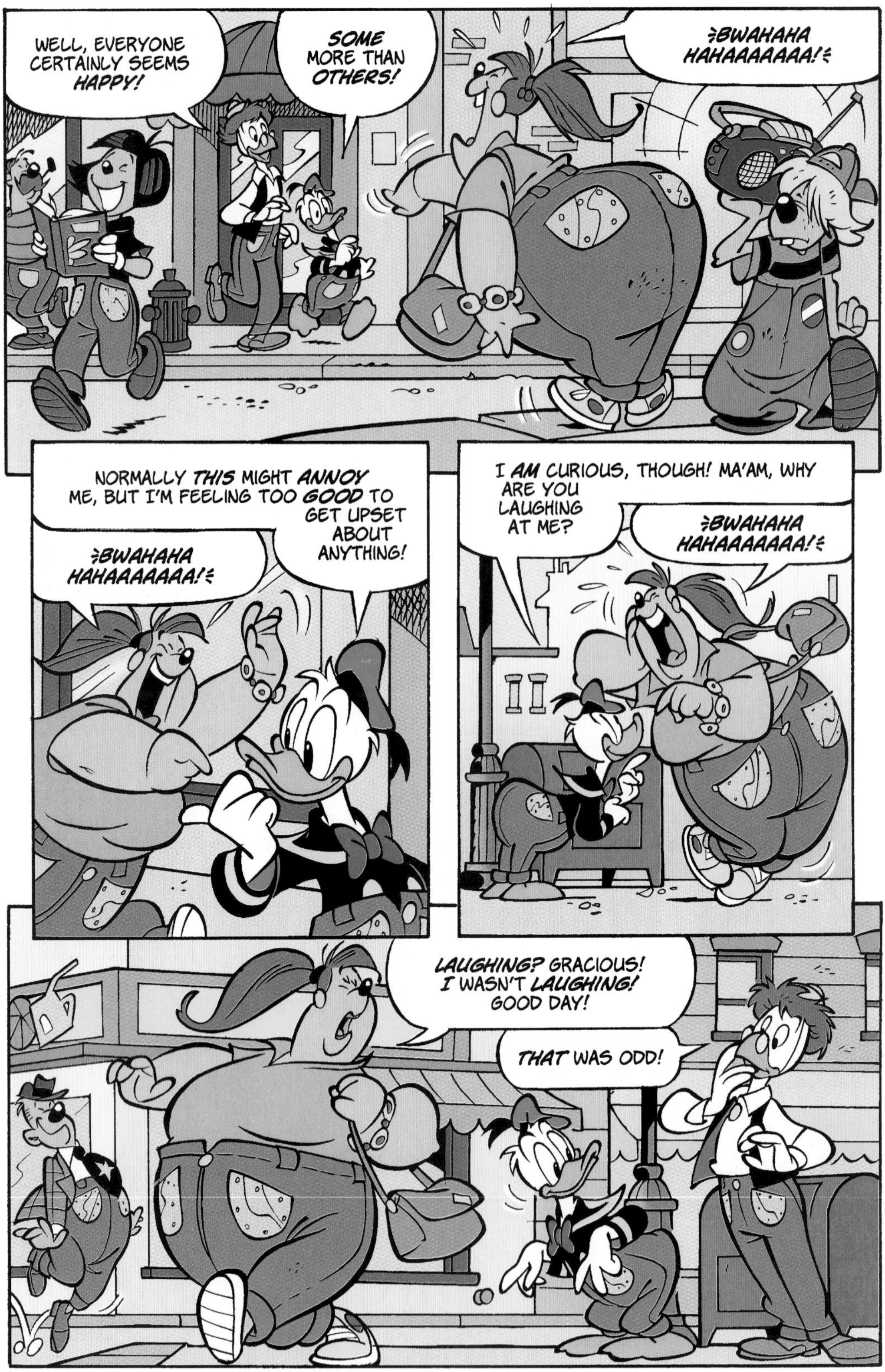
WELL, EVERYONE CERTAINLY SEEMS HAPPY!
SOME MORE THAN OTHERS!
BWAHAHA HAHAAAAAAAA!
NORMALLY THIS MIGHT ANNOY ME, BUT I'M FEELING TOO GOOD TO GET UPSET ABOUT ANYTHING!
BWAHAHA HAHAAAAAAAA!
I AM CURIOUS, THOUGH! MA'AM, WHY ARE YOU LAUGHING AT ME?
BWAHAHA HAHAAAAAAAA!
LAUGHING? GRACIOUS! I WASN'T LAUGHING! GOOD DAY!
THAT WAS ODD!

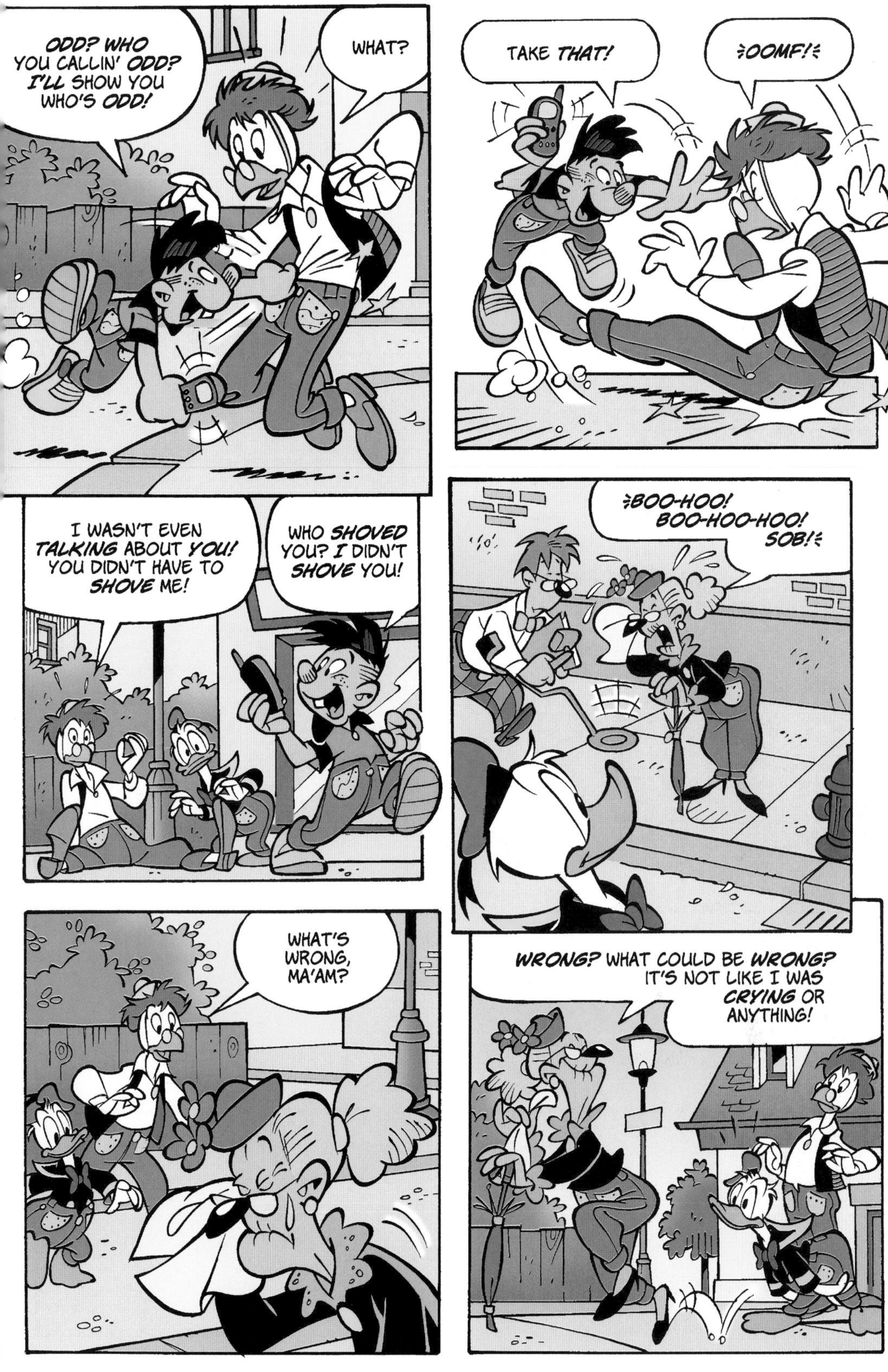
ODD? WHO YOU CALLIN' ODD? I'LL SHOW YOU WHO'S ODD!
WHAT?
TAKE THAT!
OOMF!
I WASN'T EVEN TALKING ABOUT YOU! YOU DIDN'T HAVE TO SHOVE ME!
WHO SHOVED YOU? I DIDN'T SHOVE YOU!
BOO-HOO! BOO-HOO-HOO! SOB!
WHAT'S WRONG, MA'AM?
WRONG? WHAT COULD BE WRONG? IT'S NOT LIKE I WAS CRYING OR ANYTHING!

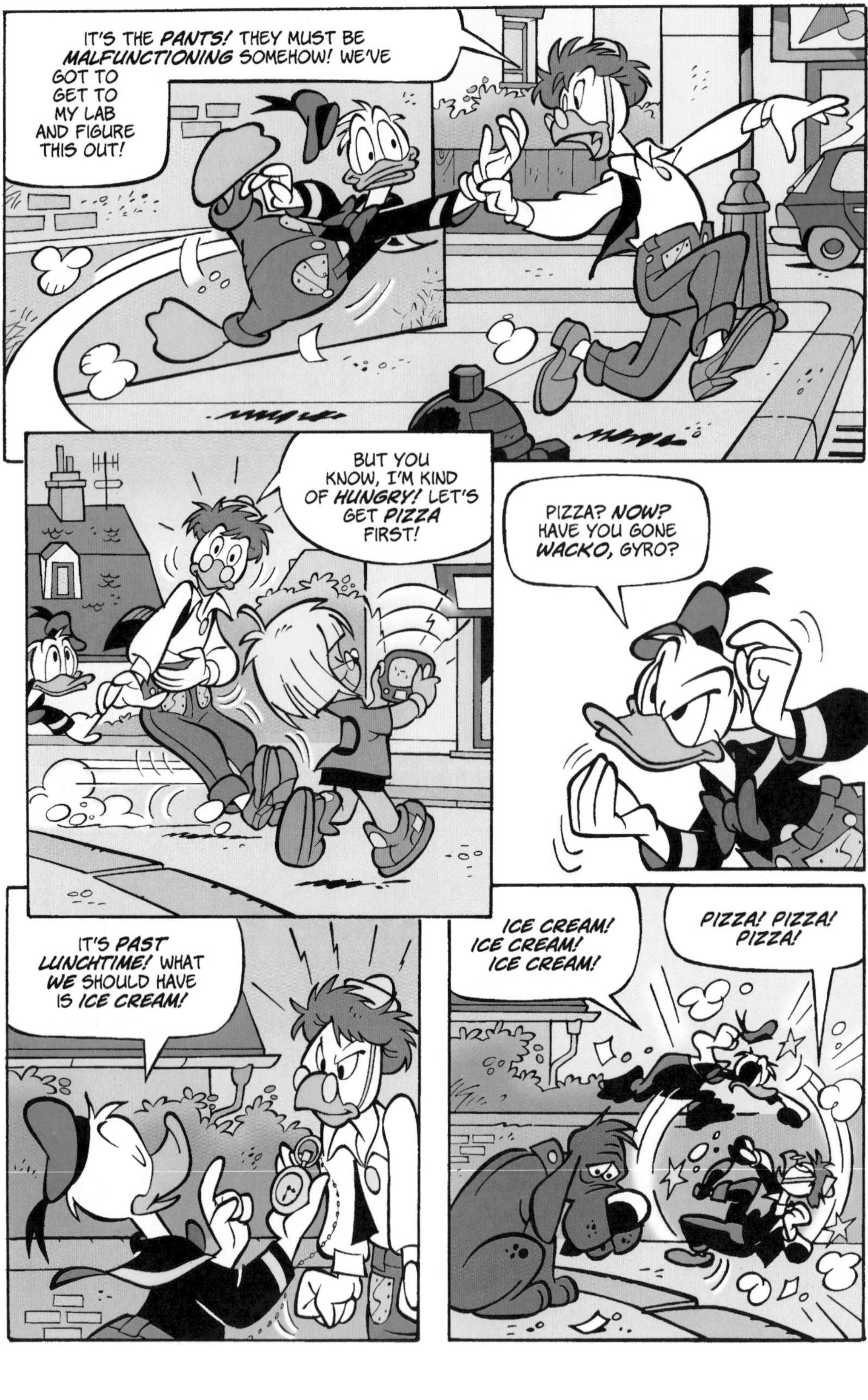

IT'S THE PANTS! THEY MUST BE MALFUNCTIONING SOMEHOW! WE'VE GOT TO GET TO MY LAB AND FIGURE THIS OUT!
BUT YOU KNOW, I'M KIND OF HUNGRY! LET'S GET PIZZA FIRST!
PIZZA? NOW? HAVE YOU GONE WACKO, GYRO?
IT'S PAST LUNCHTIME! WHAT WE SHOULD HAVE IS ICE CREAM!
ICE CREAM! ICE CREAM! ICE CREAM!
PIZZA! PIZZA! PIZZA!

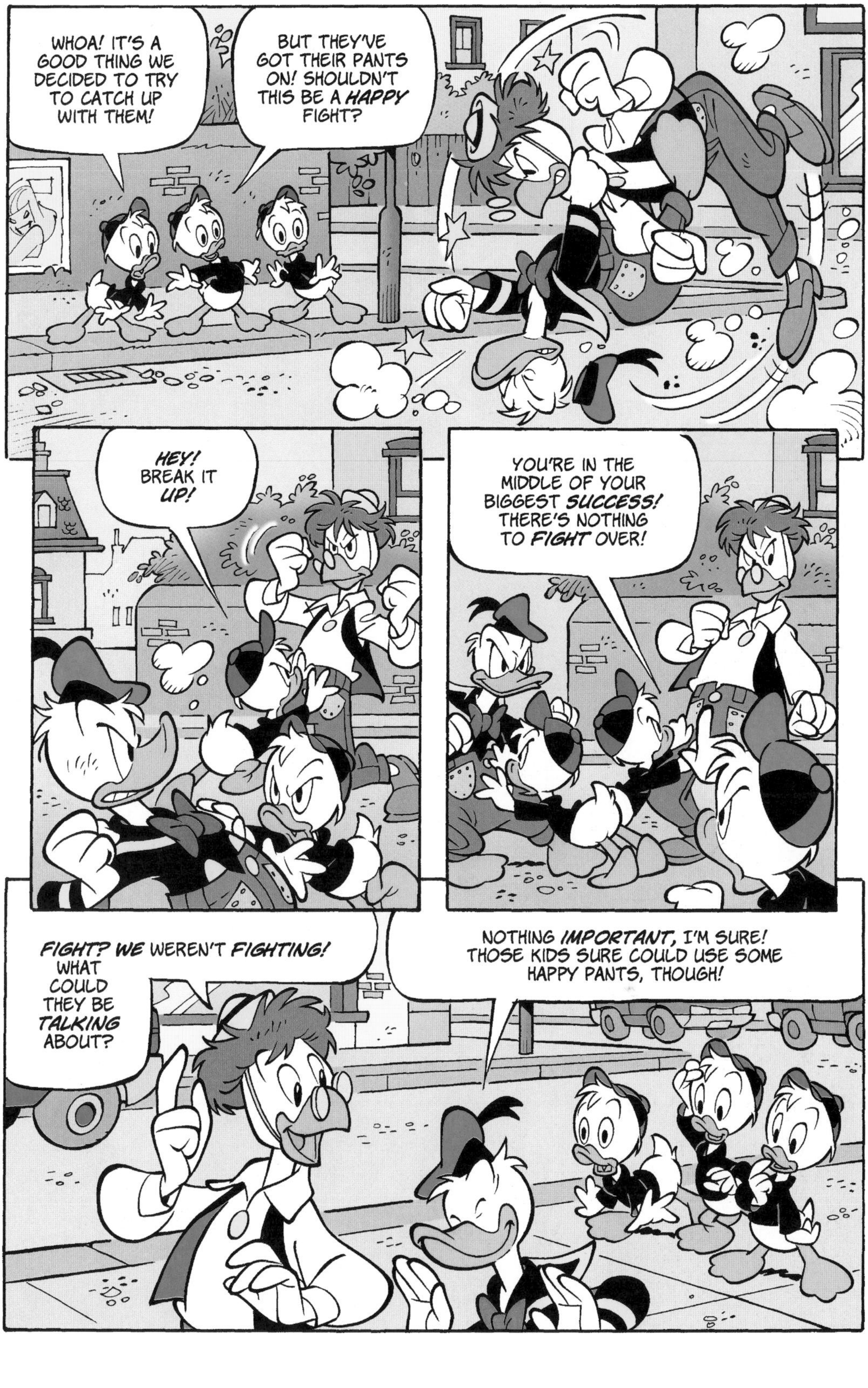
WHOA! IT'S A GOOD THING WE DECIDED TO TRY TO CATCH UP WITH THEM!
BUT THEY'VE GOT THEIR PANTS ON! SHOULDN'T THIS BE A HAPPY FIGHT?
HEY! BREAK IT UP!
YOU'RE IN THE MIDDLE OF YOUR BIGGEST SUCCESS! THERE'S NOTHING TO FIGHT OVER!
FIGHT? WE WEREN'T FIGHTING! WHAT COULD THEY BE TALKING ABOUT?
NOTHING IMPORTANT, I'M SURE! THOSE KIDS SURE COULD USE SOME HAPPY PANTS, THOUGH!

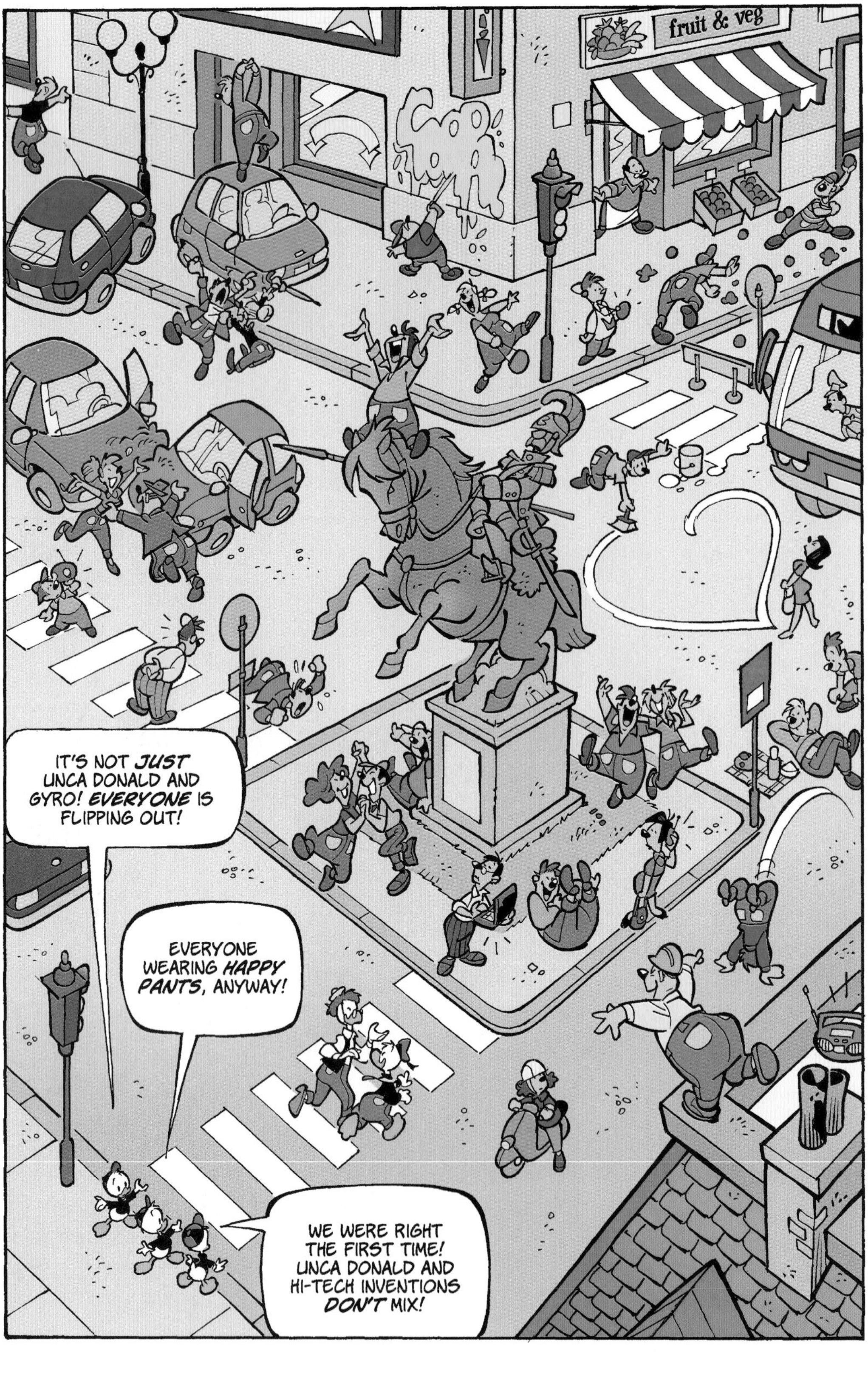
fruit & veg
IT'S NOT *JUST* UNCA DONALD AND GYRO! *EVERYONE* IS FLIPPING OUT!
EVERYONE WEARING *HAPPY PANTS*, ANYWAY!
WE WERE RIGHT THE FIRST TIME! UNCA DONALD AND HI-TECH INVENTIONS *DON'T* MIX!

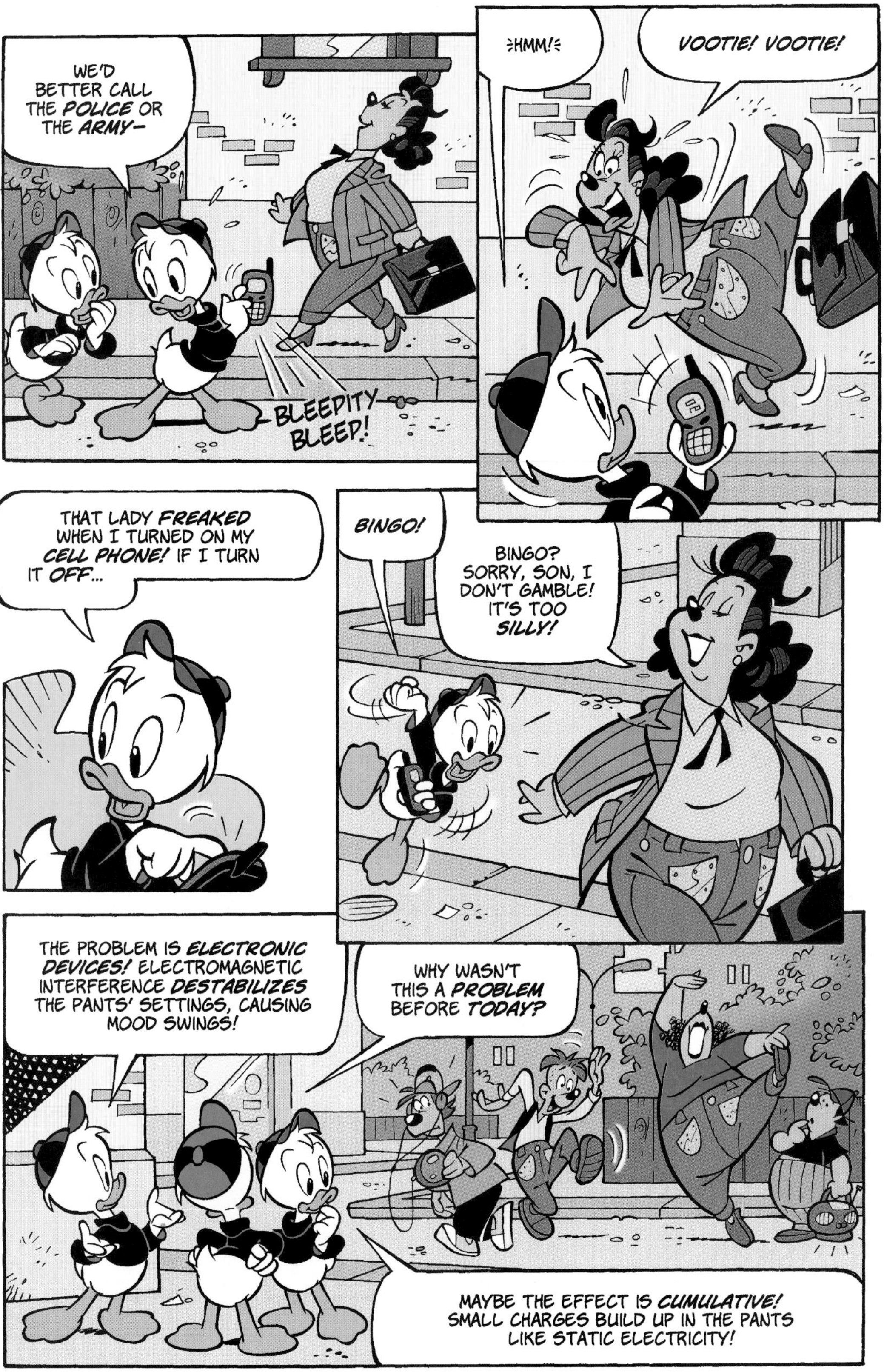
WE'D BETTER CALL THE POLICE OR THE ARMY—
BLEEPITY BLEEP!
HMM!
VOOTIE! VOOTIE!
THAT LADY FREAKED WHEN I TURNED ON MY CELL PHONE! IF I TURN IT OFF...
BINGO!
BINGO? SORRY, SON, I DON'T GAMBLE! IT'S TOO SILLY!
THE PROBLEM IS ELECTRONIC DEVICES! ELECTROMAGNETIC INTERFERENCE DESTABILIZES THE PANTS' SETTINGS, CAUSING MOOD SWINGS!
WHY WASN'T THIS A PROBLEM BEFORE TODAY?
MAYBE THE EFFECT IS CUMULATIVE! SMALL CHARGES BUILD UP IN THE PANTS LIKE STATIC ELECTRICITY!

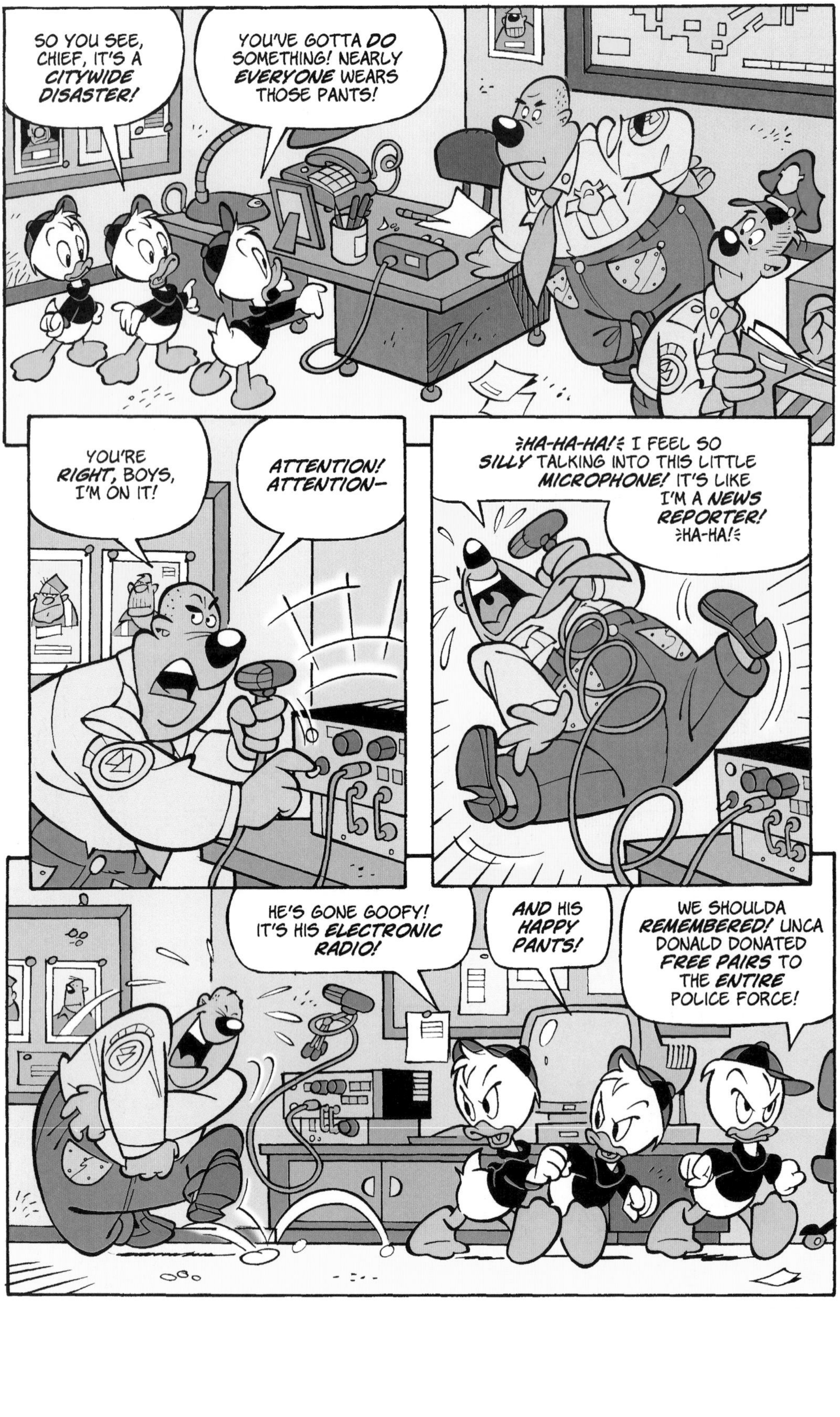
SO YOU SEE, CHIEF, IT'S A *CITYWIDE DISASTER!*
YOU'VE GOTTA *DO* SOMETHING! NEARLY *EVERYONE* WEARS THOSE PANTS!
YOU'RE *RIGHT*, BOYS, I'M ON IT!
ATTENTION! ATTENTION—
HA-HA-HA! I FEEL SO *SILLY* TALKING INTO THIS LITTLE *MICROPHONE!* IT'S LIKE I'M A *NEWS REPORTER!* HA-HA!
HE'S GONE GOOFY! IT'S HIS *ELECTRONIC RADIO!*
AND HIS *HAPPY PANTS!*
WE SHOULDA *REMEMBERED!* UNCA DONALD DONATED *FREE PAIRS* TO THE *ENTIRE* POLICE FORCE!

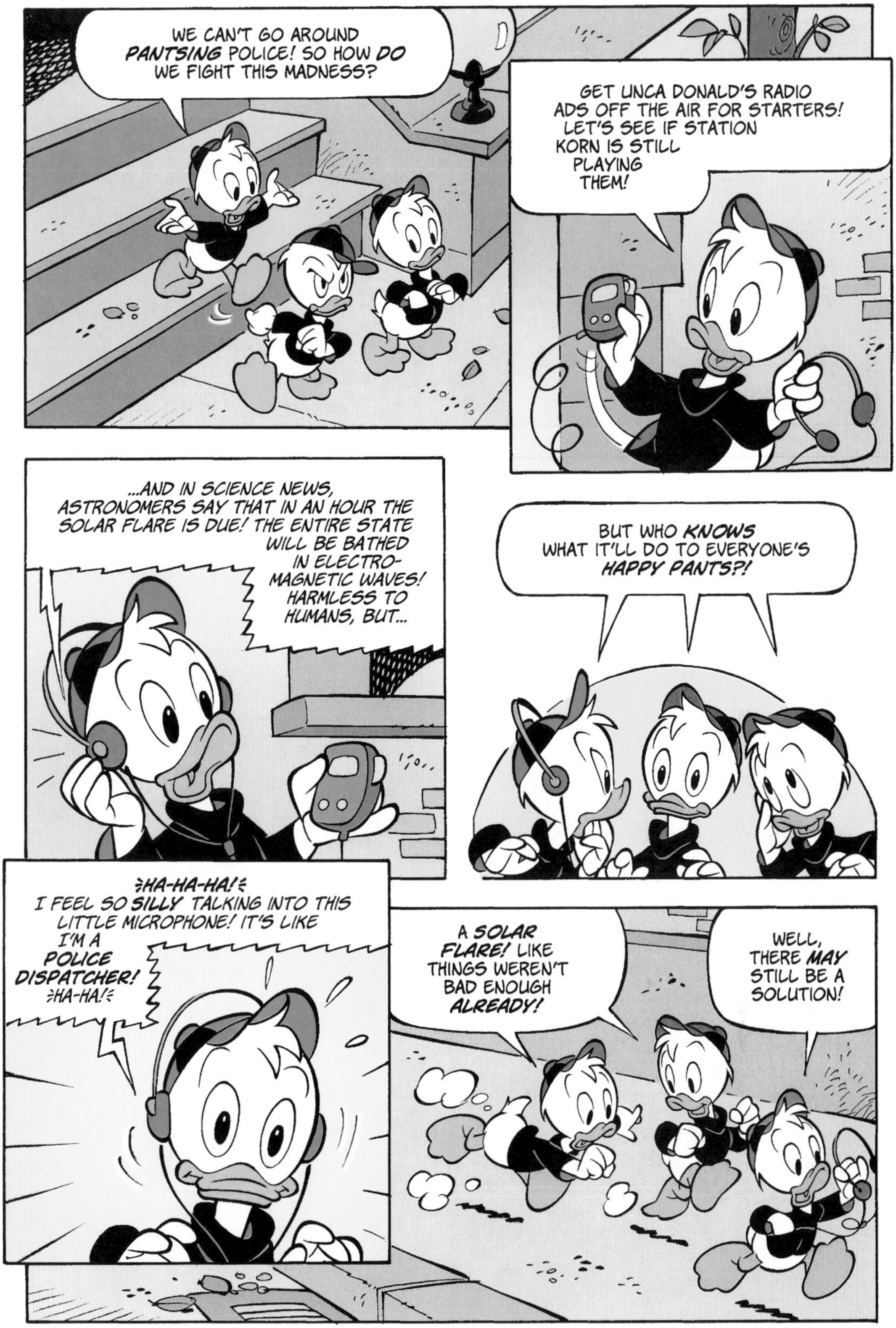
WE CAN'T GO AROUND PANTSING POLICE! SO HOW DO WE FIGHT THIS MADNESS?
GET UNCA DONALD'S RADIO ADS OFF THE AIR FOR STARTERS! LET'S SEE IF STATION KORN IS STILL PLAYING THEM!
...AND IN SCIENCE NEWS, ASTRONOMERS SAY THAT IN AN HOUR THE SOLAR FLARE IS DUE! THE ENTIRE STATE WILL BE BATHED IN ELECTRO-MAGNETIC WAVES! HARMLESS TO HUMANS, BUT...
BUT WHO KNOWS WHAT IT'LL DO TO EVERYONE'S HAPPY PANTS?!
HA-HA-HA! I FEEL SO SILLY TALKING INTO THIS LITTLE MICROPHONE! IT'S LIKE I'M A POLICE DISPATCHER! HA-HA!
A SOLAR FLARE! LIKE THINGS WEREN'T BAD ENOUGH ALREADY!
WELL, THERE MAY STILL BE A SOLUTION!

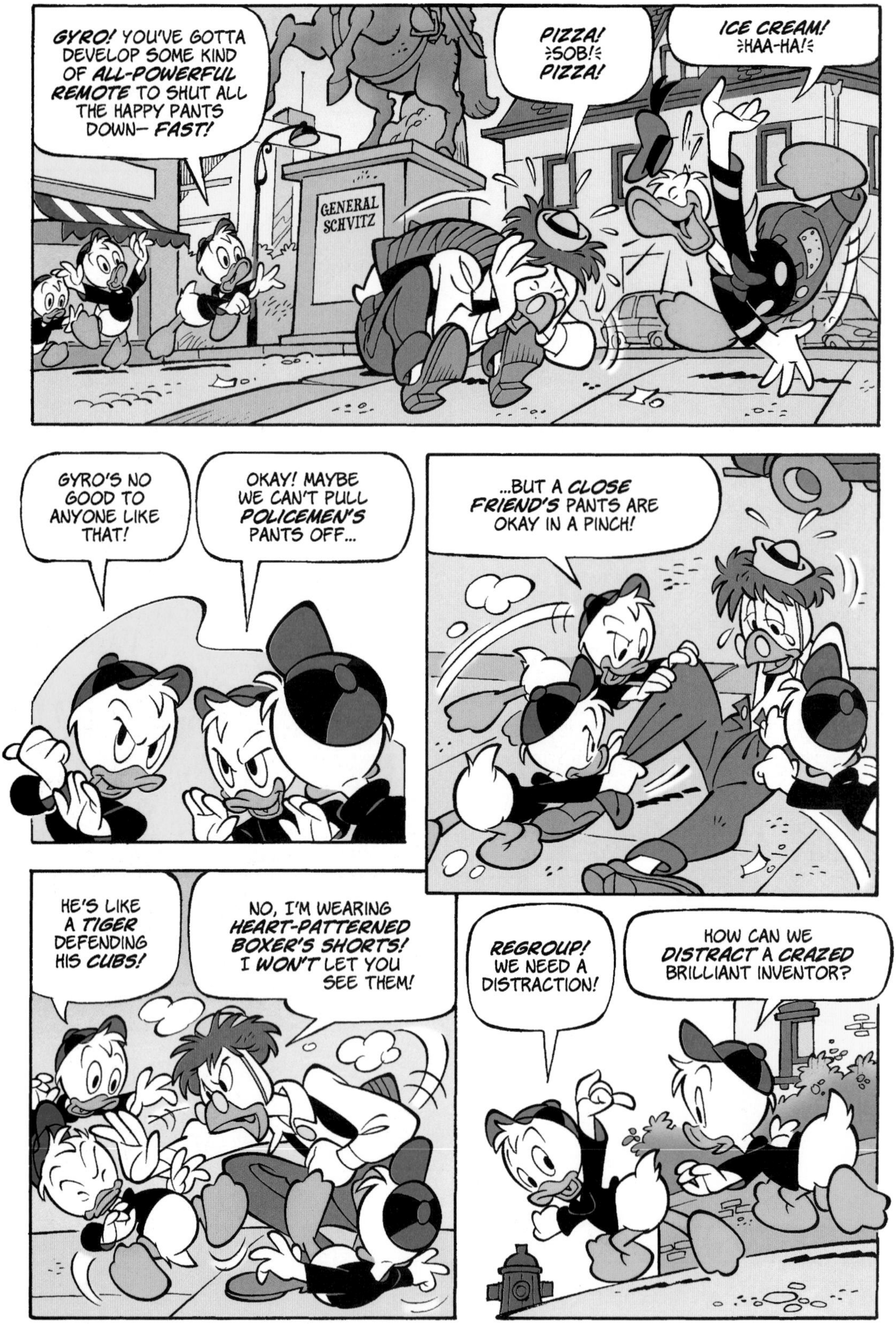
GYRO! YOU'VE GOTTA DEVELOP SOME KIND OF ALL-POWERFUL REMOTE TO SHUT ALL THE HAPPY PANTS DOWN— FAST!
GENERAL SCHVITZ
PIZZA! SOB! PIZZA!
ICE CREAM! HAA-HA!
GYRO'S NO GOOD TO ANYONE LIKE THAT!
OKAY! MAYBE WE CAN'T PULL POLICEMEN'S PANTS OFF...
...BUT A CLOSE FRIEND'S PANTS ARE OKAY IN A PINCH!
HE'S LIKE A TIGER DEFENDING HIS CUBS!
NO, I'M WEARING HEART-PATTERNED BOXER'S SHORTS! I WON'T LET YOU SEE THEM!
REGROUP! WE NEED A DISTRACTION!
HOW CAN WE DISTRACT A CRAZED BRILLIANT INVENTOR?

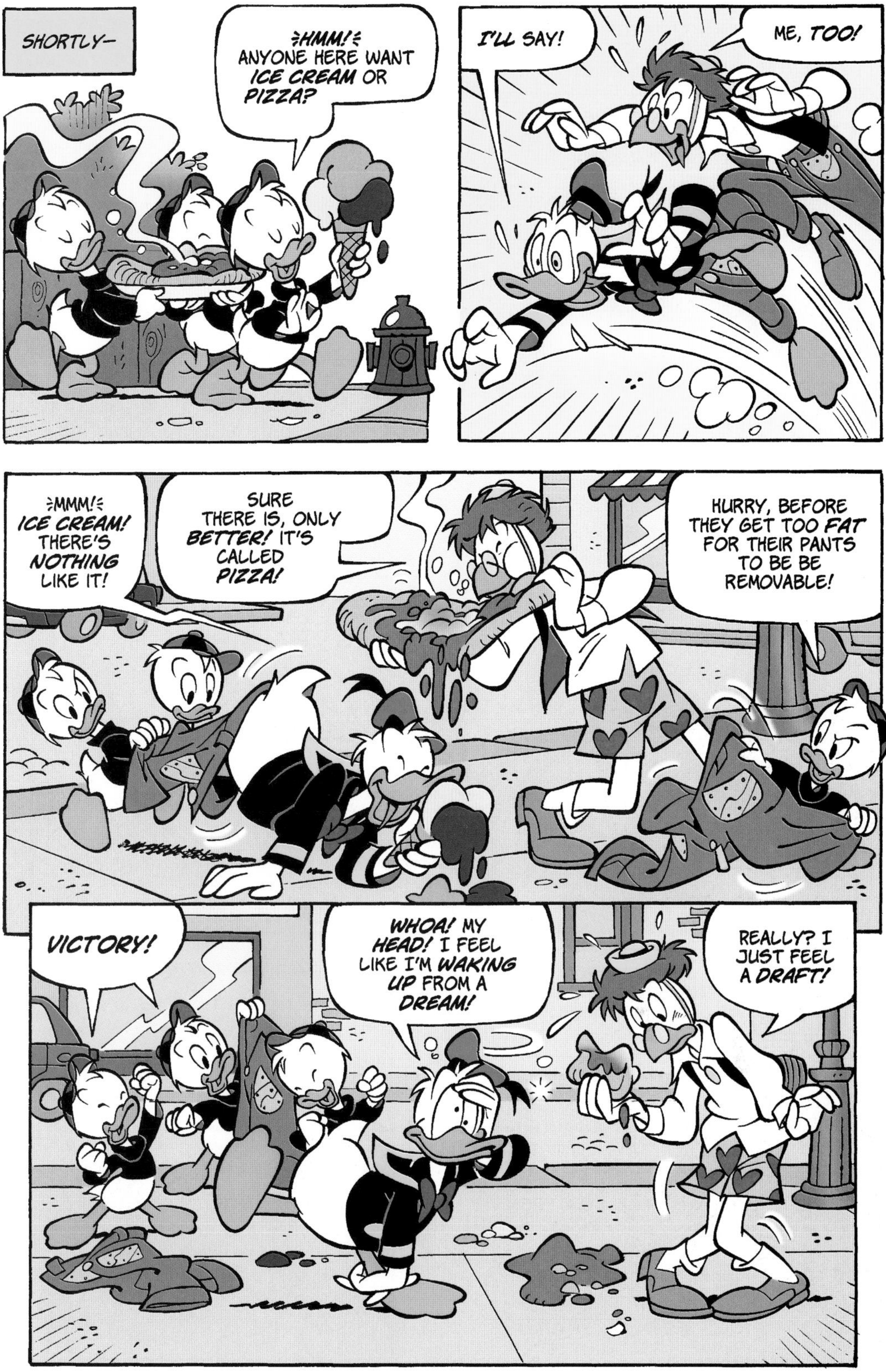
SHORTLY—
≈HMM!≈ ANYONE HERE WANT ICE CREAM OR PIZZA?
I'LL SAY!
ME, TOO!
≈MMM!≈ ICE CREAM! THERE'S NOTHING LIKE IT!
SURE THERE IS, ONLY BETTER! IT'S CALLED PIZZA!
HURRY, BEFORE THEY GET TOO FAT FOR THEIR PANTS TO BE BE REMOVABLE!
VICTORY!
WHOA! MY HEAD! I FEEL LIKE I'M WAKING UP FROM A DREAM!
REALLY? I JUST FEEL A DRAFT!

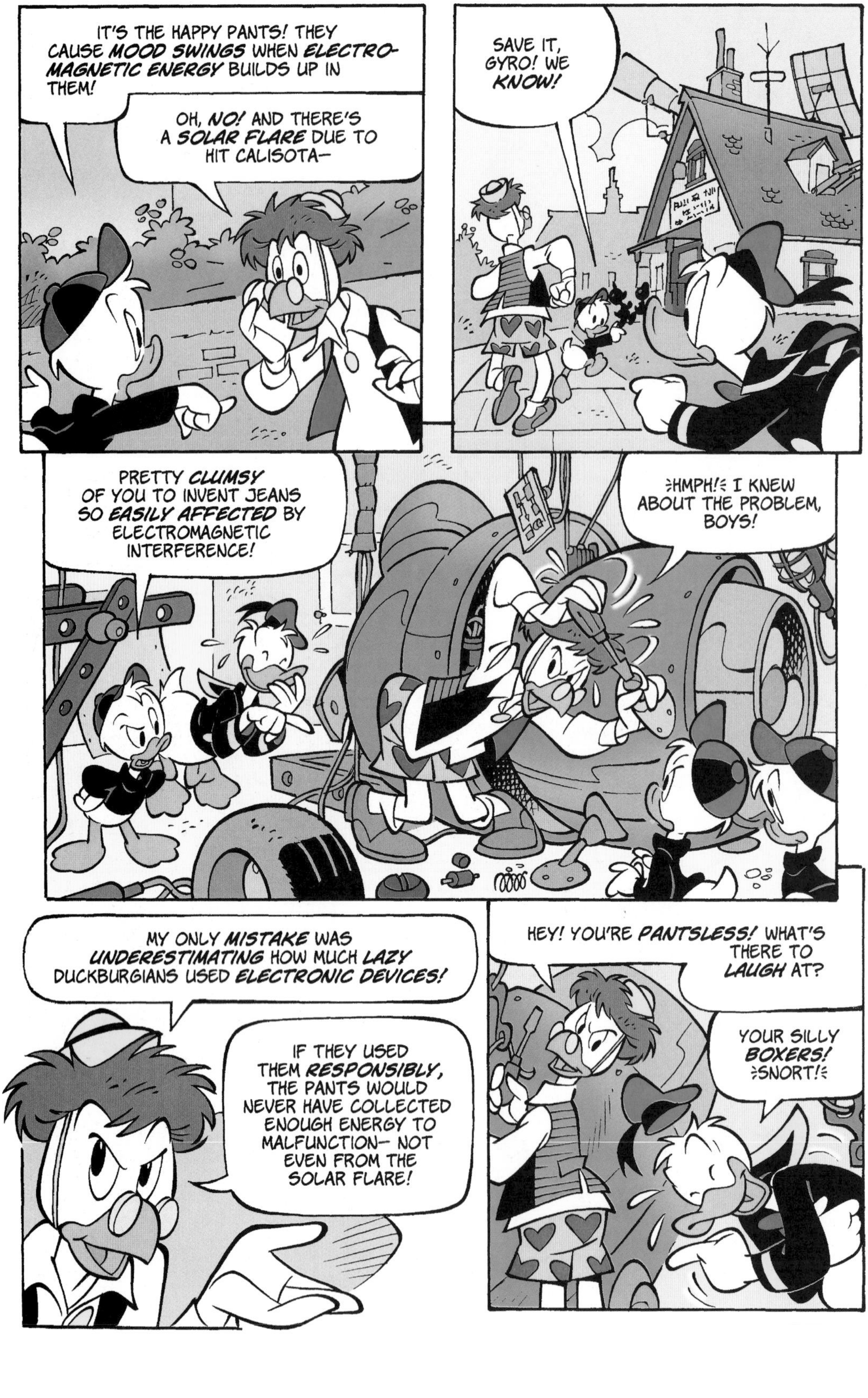
IT'S THE HAPPY PANTS! THEY CAUSE MOOD SWINGS WHEN ELECTROMAGNETIC ENERGY BUILDS UP IN THEM!
OH, NO! AND THERE'S A SOLAR FLARE DUE TO HIT CALISOTA—
SAVE IT, GYRO! WE KNOW!
PRETTY CLUMSY OF YOU TO INVENT JEANS SO EASILY AFFECTED BY ELECTROMAGNETIC INTERFERENCE!
HMPH! I KNEW ABOUT THE PROBLEM, BOYS!
MY ONLY MISTAKE WAS UNDERESTIMATING HOW MUCH LAZY DUCKBURGIANS USED ELECTRONIC DEVICES!
IF THEY USED THEM RESPONSIBLY, THE PANTS WOULD NEVER HAVE COLLECTED ENOUGH ENERGY TO MALFUNCTION— NOT EVEN FROM THE SOLAR FLARE!
HEY! YOU'RE PANTSLESS! WHAT'S THERE TO LAUGH AT?
YOUR SILLY BOXERS! SNORT!

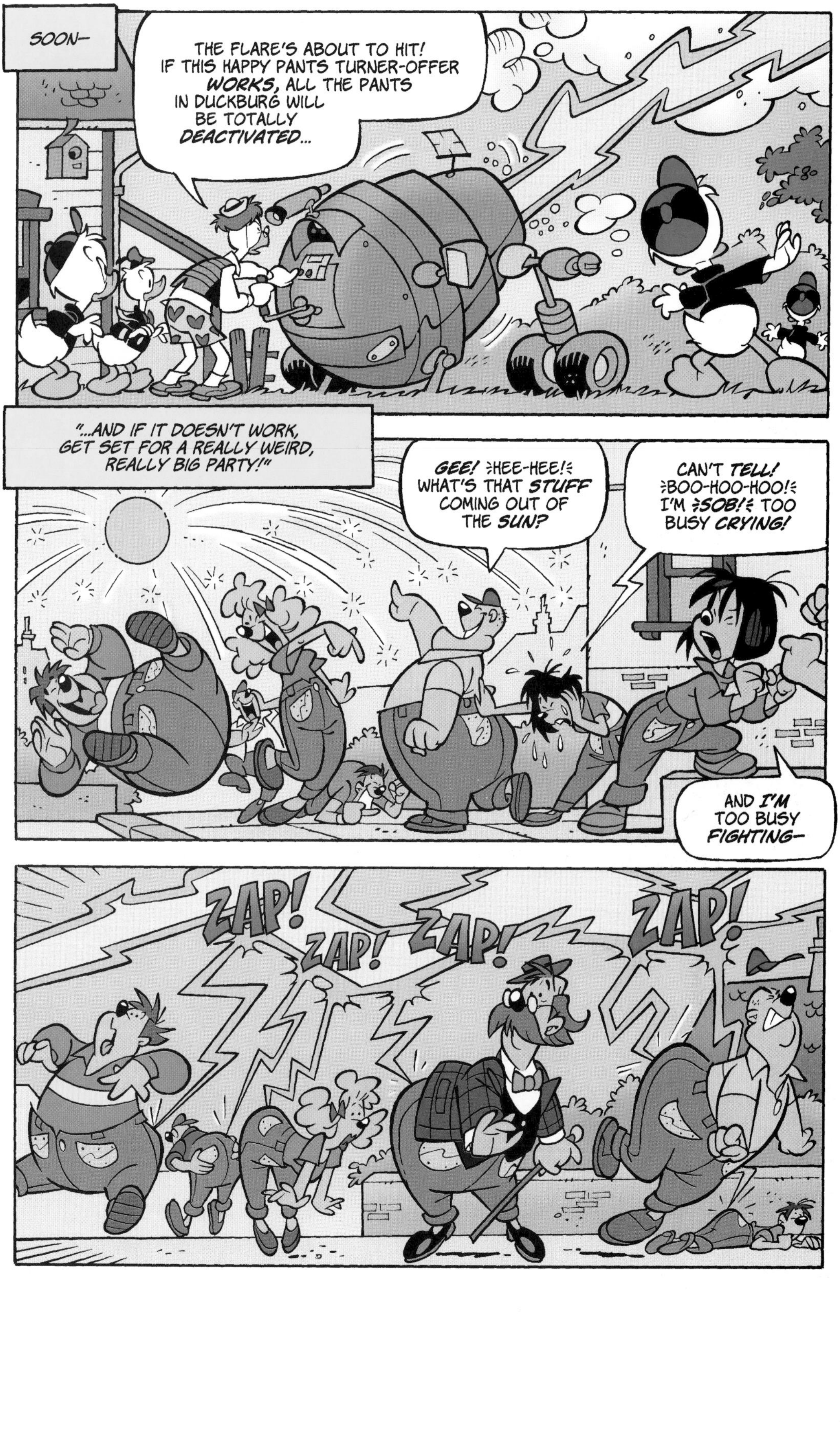
SOON—
THE FLARE'S ABOUT TO HIT! IF THIS HAPPY PANTS TURNER-OFFER WORKS, ALL THE PANTS IN DUCKBURG WILL BE TOTALLY DEACTIVATED...
"...AND IF IT DOESN'T WORK, GET SET FOR A REALLY WEIRD, REALLY BIG PARTY!"
GEE! HEE-HEE! WHAT'S THAT STUFF COMING OUT OF THE SUN?
CAN'T TELL! BOO-HOO-HOO! I'M SOB! TOO BUSY CRYING!
AND I'M TOO BUSY FIGHTING—
ZAP!
ZAP!
ZAP!
ZAP!

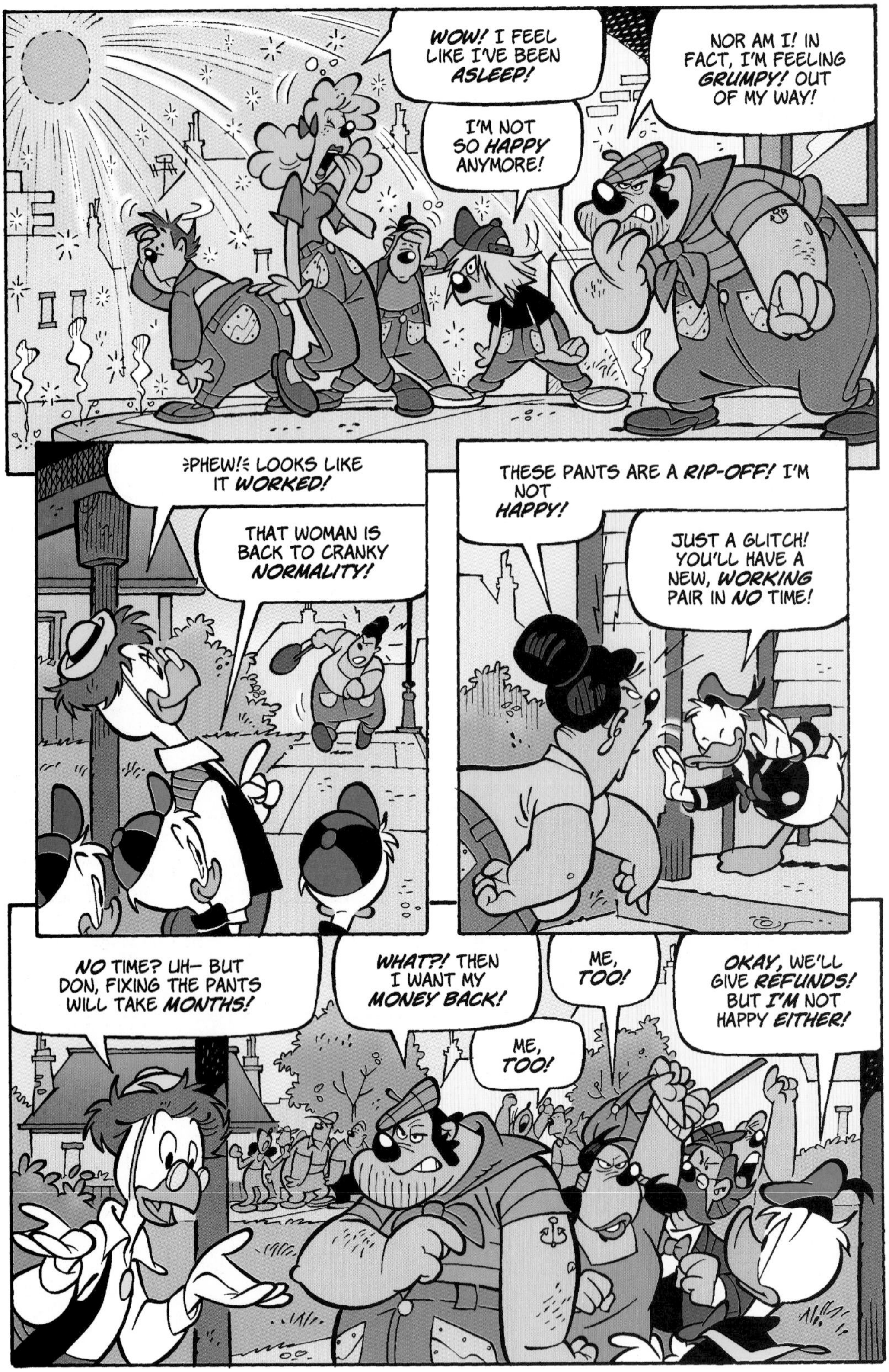

WOW! I FEEL LIKE I'VE BEEN ASLEEP!
I'M NOT SO HAPPY ANYMORE!
NOR AM I! IN FACT, I'M FEELING GRUMPY! OUT OF MY WAY!
PHEW! LOOKS LIKE IT WORKED!
THAT WOMAN IS BACK TO CRANKY NORMALITY!
THESE PANTS ARE A RIP-OFF! I'M NOT HAPPY!
JUST A GLITCH! YOU'LL HAVE A NEW, WORKING PAIR IN NO TIME!
NO TIME? UH— BUT DON, FIXING THE PANTS WILL TAKE MONTHS!
WHAT?! THEN I WANT MY MONEY BACK!
ME, TOO!
ME, TOO!
OKAY, WE'LL GIVE REFUNDS! BUT I'M NOT HAPPY EITHER!

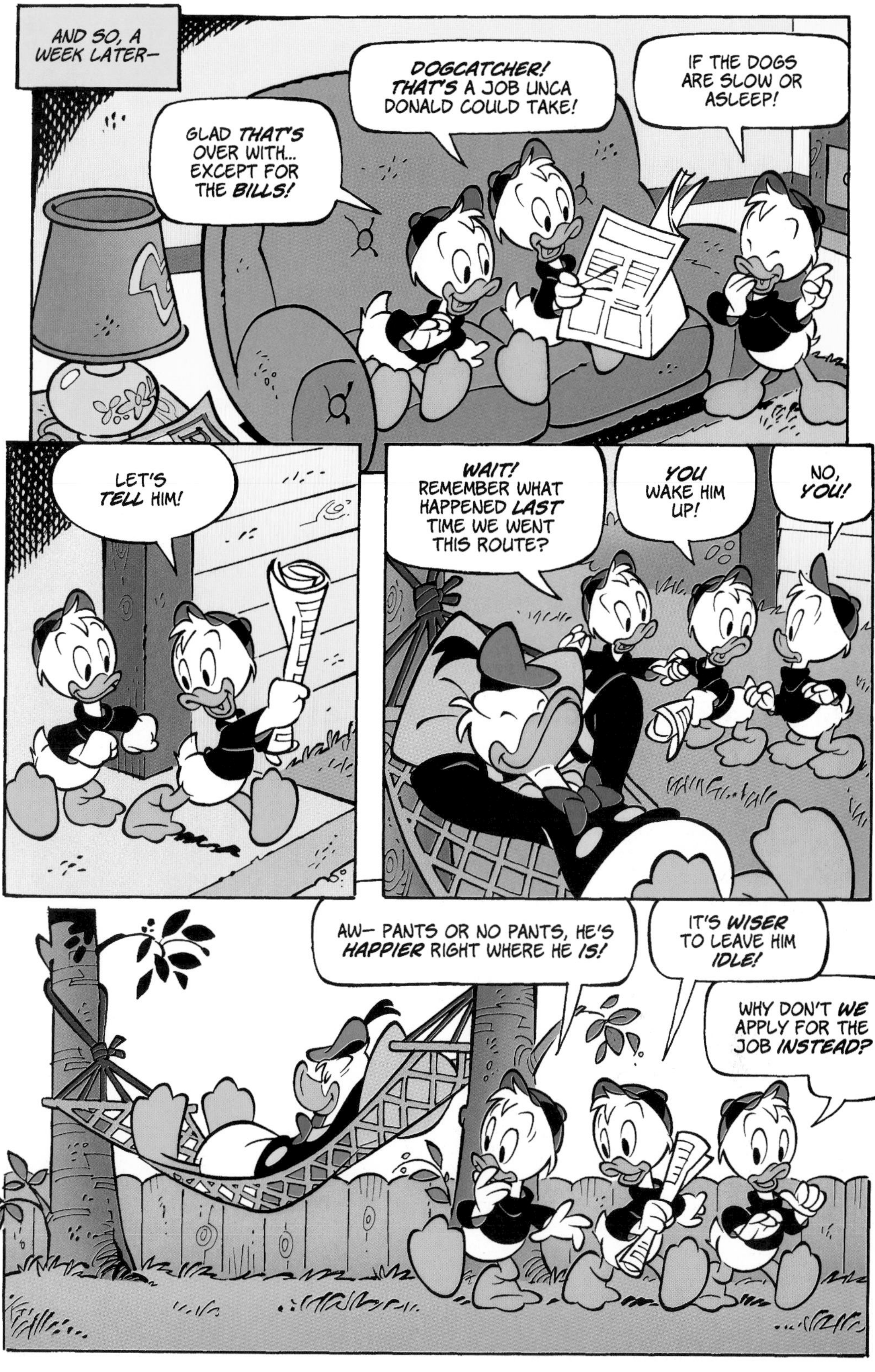
AND SO, A WEEK LATER—
GLAD THAT'S OVER WITH... EXCEPT FOR THE BILLS!
DOGCATCHER! THAT'S A JOB UNCA DONALD COULD TAKE!
IF THE DOGS ARE SLOW OR ASLEEP!
LET'S TELL HIM!
WAIT! REMEMBER WHAT HAPPENED LAST TIME WE WENT THIS ROUTE?
YOU WAKE HIM UP!
NO, YOU!
AW— PANTS OR NO PANTS, HE'S HAPPIER RIGHT WHERE HE IS!
IT'S WISER TO LEAVE HIM IDLE!
WHY DON'T WE APPLY FOR THE JOB INSTEAD?

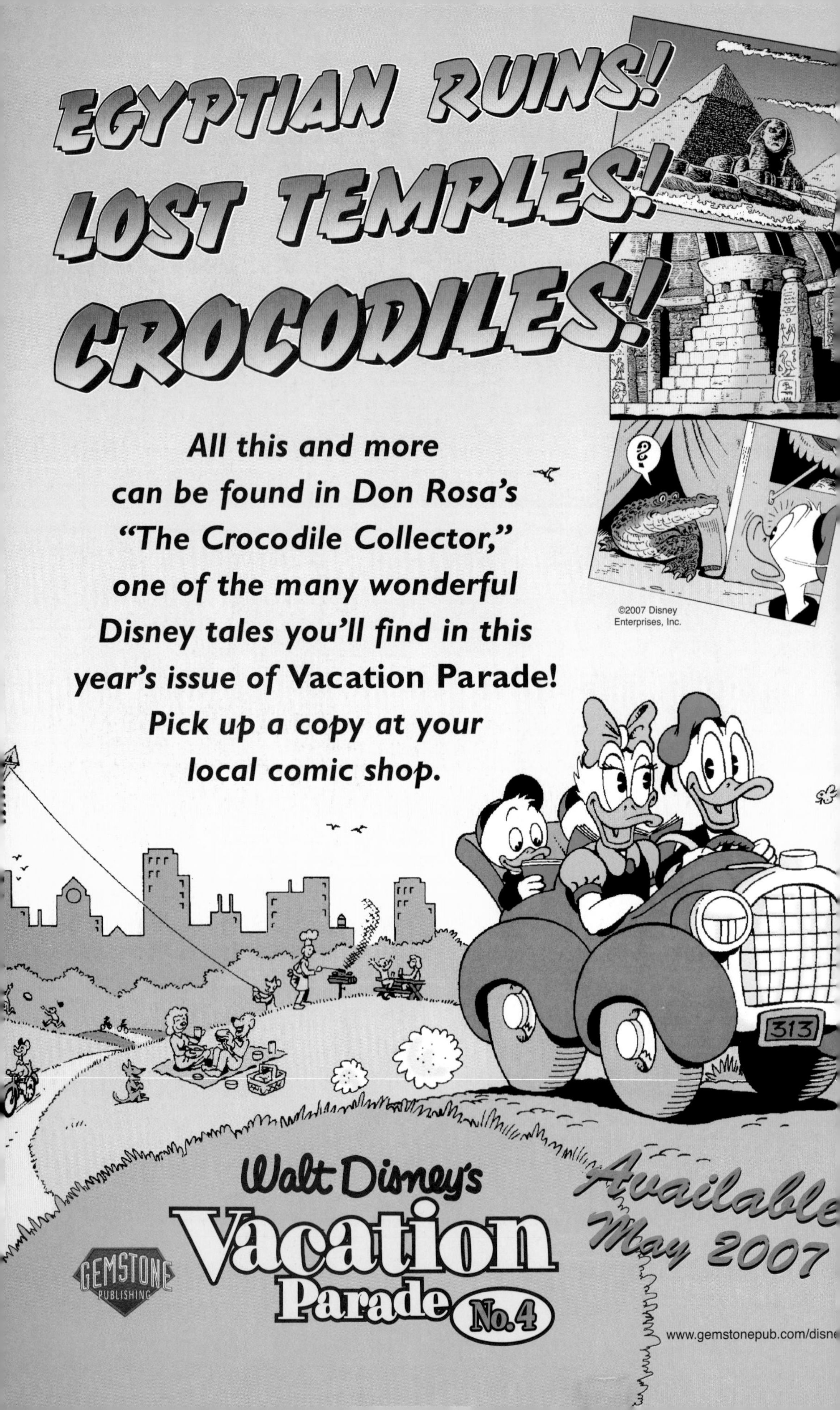
EGYPTIAN RUINS!
LOST TEMPLES!
CROCODILES!
All this and more can be found in Don Rosa's "The Crocodile Collector," one of the many wonderful Disney tales you'll find in this year's issue of Vacation Parade! Pick up a copy at your local comic shop.
©2007 Disney Enterprises, Inc.
313
GEMSTONE PUBLISHING
Walt Disney's Vacation Parade No. 4
Available May 2007
www.gemstonepub.com/disn

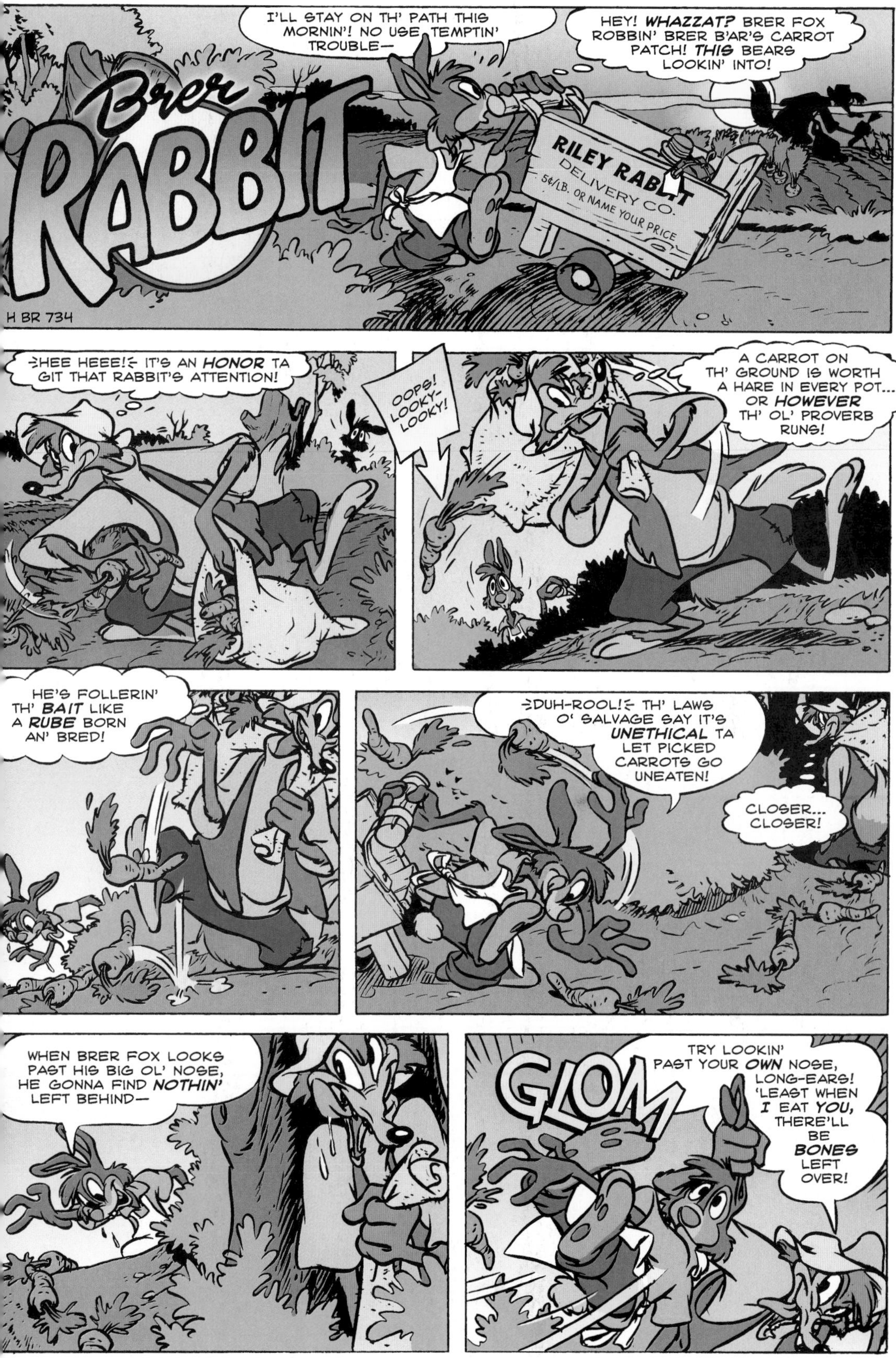

Brer RABBIT
I'LL STAY ON TH' PATH THIS MORNIN'! NO USE TEMPTIN' TROUBLE—
HEY! WHAZZAT? BRER FOX ROBBIN' BRER B'AR'S CARROT PATCH! THIS BEARS LOOKIN' INTO!
RILEY RABBIT DELIVERY CO. 5¢/LB. OR NAME YOUR PRICE
H BR 734
HEE HEEE! IT'S AN HONOR TA GIT THAT RABBIT'S ATTENTION!
OOPS! LOOKY-LOOKY!
A CARROT ON TH' GROUND IS WORTH A HARE IN EVERY POT... OR HOWEVER TH' OL' PROVERB RUNS!
HE'S FOLLERIN' TH' BAIT LIKE A RUBE BORN AN' BRED!
DUH-ROOL! TH' LAWS O' SALVAGE SAY IT'S UNETHICAL TA LET PICKED CARROTS GO UNEATEN!
CLOSER... CLOSER!
WHEN BRER FOX LOOKS PAST HIS BIG OL' NOSE, HE GONNA FIND NOTHIN' LEFT BEHIND—
GLOM
TRY LOOKIN' PAST YOUR OWN NOSE, LONG-EARS! 'LEAST WHEN I EAT YOU, THERE'LL BE BONES LEFT OVER!

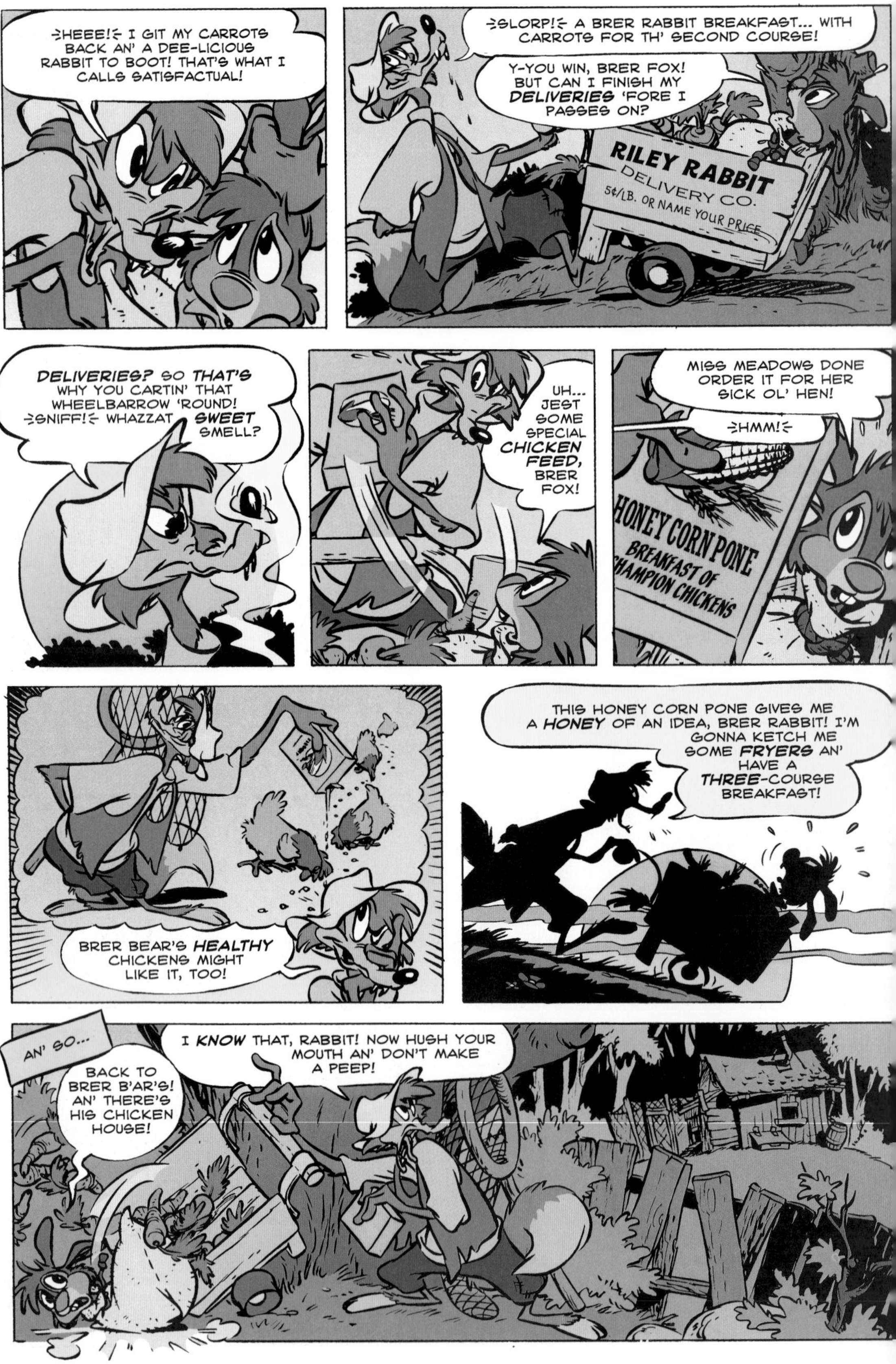

⇒HEEE!⇐ I GIT MY CARROTS BACK AN' A DEE-LICIOUS RABBIT TO BOOT! THAT'S WHAT I CALLS SATISFACTUAL!
⇒SLORP!⇐ A BRER RABBIT BREAKFAST... WITH CARROTS FOR TH' SECOND COURSE!
Y-YOU WIN, BRER FOX! BUT CAN I FINISH MY DELIVERIES 'FORE I PASSES ON?
RILEY RABBIT
DELIVERY CO.
5¢/LB. OR NAME YOUR PRICE
DELIVERIES? SO THAT'S WHY YOU CARTIN' THAT WHEELBARROW 'ROUND! ⇒SNIFF!⇐ WHAZZAT SWEET SMELL?
UH... JEST SOME SPECIAL CHICKEN FEED, BRER FOX!
MISS MEADOWS DONE ORDER IT FOR HER SICK OL' HEN!
⇒HMM!⇐
HONEY CORN PONE
BREAKFAST OF CHAMPION CHICKENS
BRER BEAR'S HEALTHY CHICKENS MIGHT LIKE IT, TOO!
THIS HONEY CORN PONE GIVES ME A HONEY OF AN IDEA, BRER RABBIT! I'M GONNA KETCH ME SOME FRYERS AN' HAVE A THREE-COURSE BREAKFAST!
AN' SO...
BACK TO BRER B'AR'S! AN' THERE'S HIS CHICKEN HOUSE!
I KNOW THAT, RABBIT! NOW HUSH YOUR MOUTH AN' DON'T MAKE A PEEP!

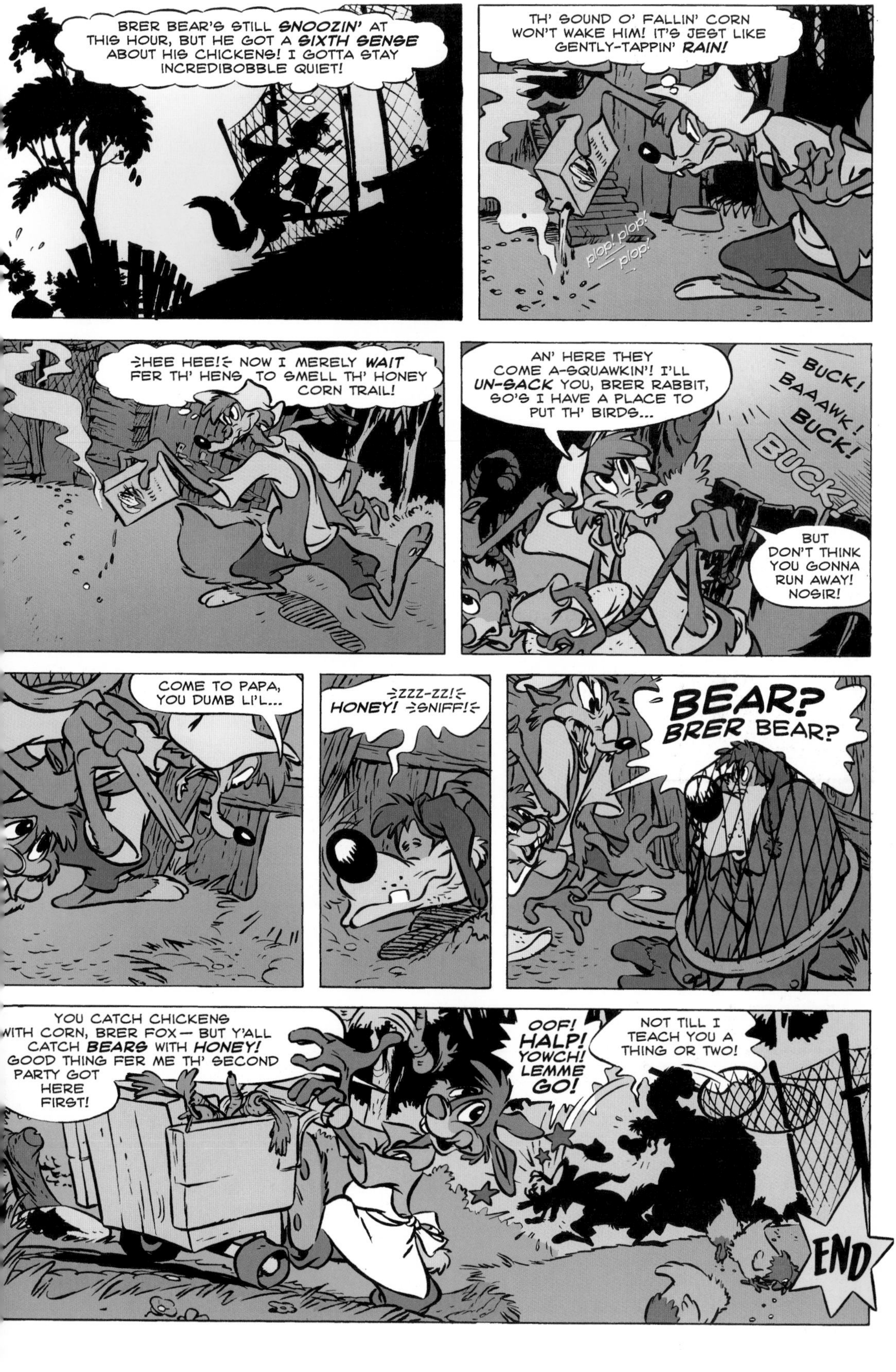
BRER BEAR'S STILL SNOOZIN' AT THIS HOUR, BUT HE GOT A SIXTH SENSE ABOUT HIS CHICKENS! I GOTTA STAY INCREDIBOBBLE QUIET!
TH' SOUND O' FALLIN' CORN WON'T WAKE HIM! IT'S JEST LIKE GENTLY-TAPPIN' RAIN!
plop! plop! plop!
HEE HEE! NOW I MERELY WAIT FER TH' HENS TO SMELL TH' HONEY CORN TRAIL!
AN' HERE THEY COME A-SQUAWKIN'! I'LL UN-SACK YOU, BRER RABBIT, SO'S I HAVE A PLACE TO PUT TH' BIRDS...
BUCK! BAAAWK! BUCK! BUCK!
BUT DON'T THINK YOU GONNA RUN AWAY! NOSIR!
COME TO PAPA, YOU DUMB LI'L...
ZZZ-ZZ! HONEY! SNIFF!
BEAR? BRER BEAR?
YOU CATCH CHICKENS WITH CORN, BRER FOX — BUT Y'ALL CATCH BEARS WITH HONEY! GOOD THING FER ME TH' SECOND PARTY GOT HERE FIRST!
OOF! HALP! YOWCH! LEMME GO!
NOT TILL I TEACH YOU A THING OR TWO!
END

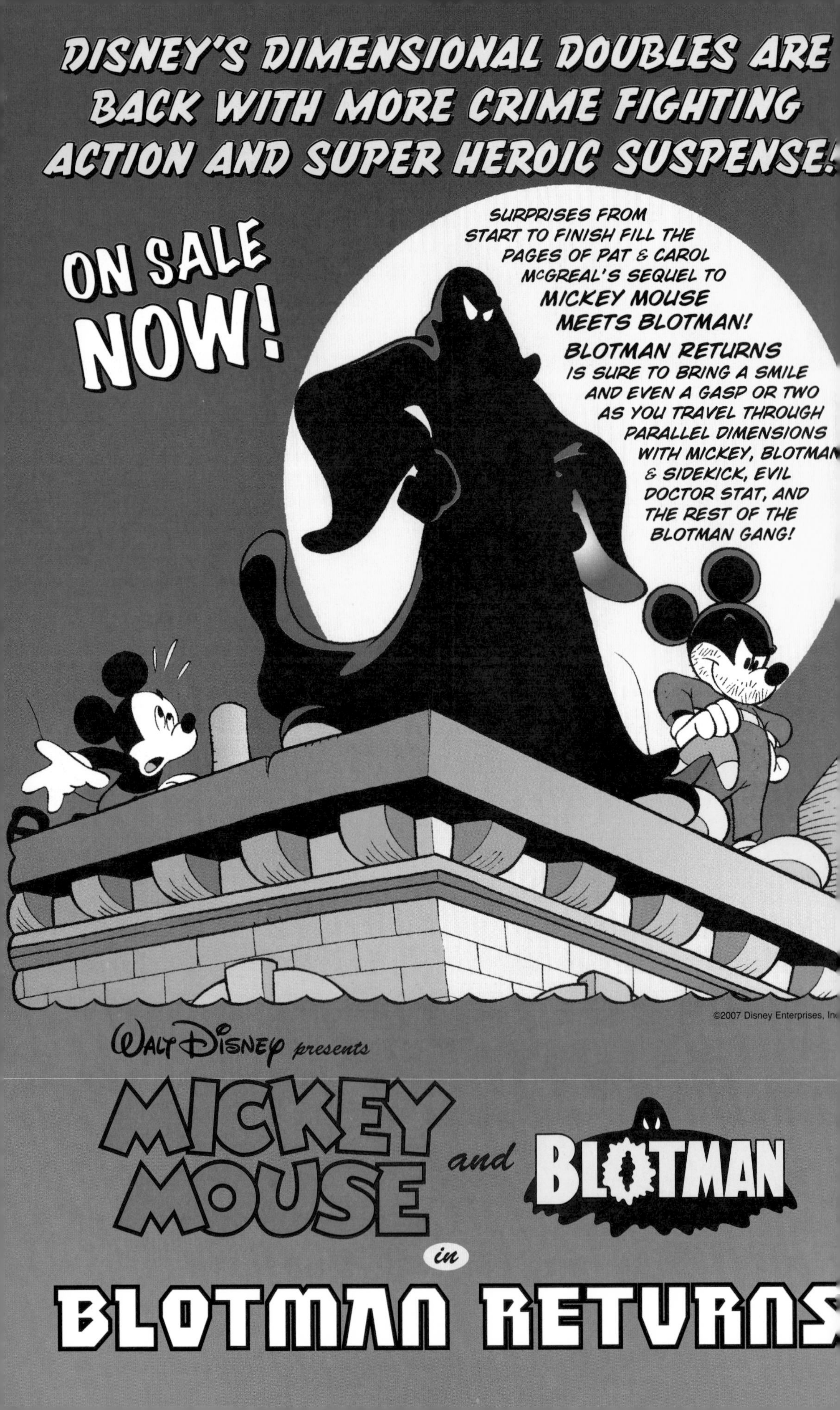

DISNEY'S DIMENSIONAL DOUBLES ARE BACK WITH MORE CRIME FIGHTING ACTION AND SUPER HEROIC SUSPENSE!
ON SALE NOW!
SURPRISES FROM START TO FINISH FILL THE PAGES OF PAT & CAROL McGREAL'S SEQUEL TO MICKEY MOUSE MEETS BLOTMAN! BLOTMAN RETURNS IS SURE TO BRING A SMILE AND EVEN A GASP OR TWO AS YOU TRAVEL THROUGH PARALLEL DIMENSIONS WITH MICKEY, BLOTMAN & SIDEKICK, EVIL DOCTOR STAT, AND THE REST OF THE BLOTMAN GANG!
©2007 Disney Enterprises, Inc
Walt Disney presents
MICKEY MOUSE and BLOTMAN
in
BLOTMAN RETURNS

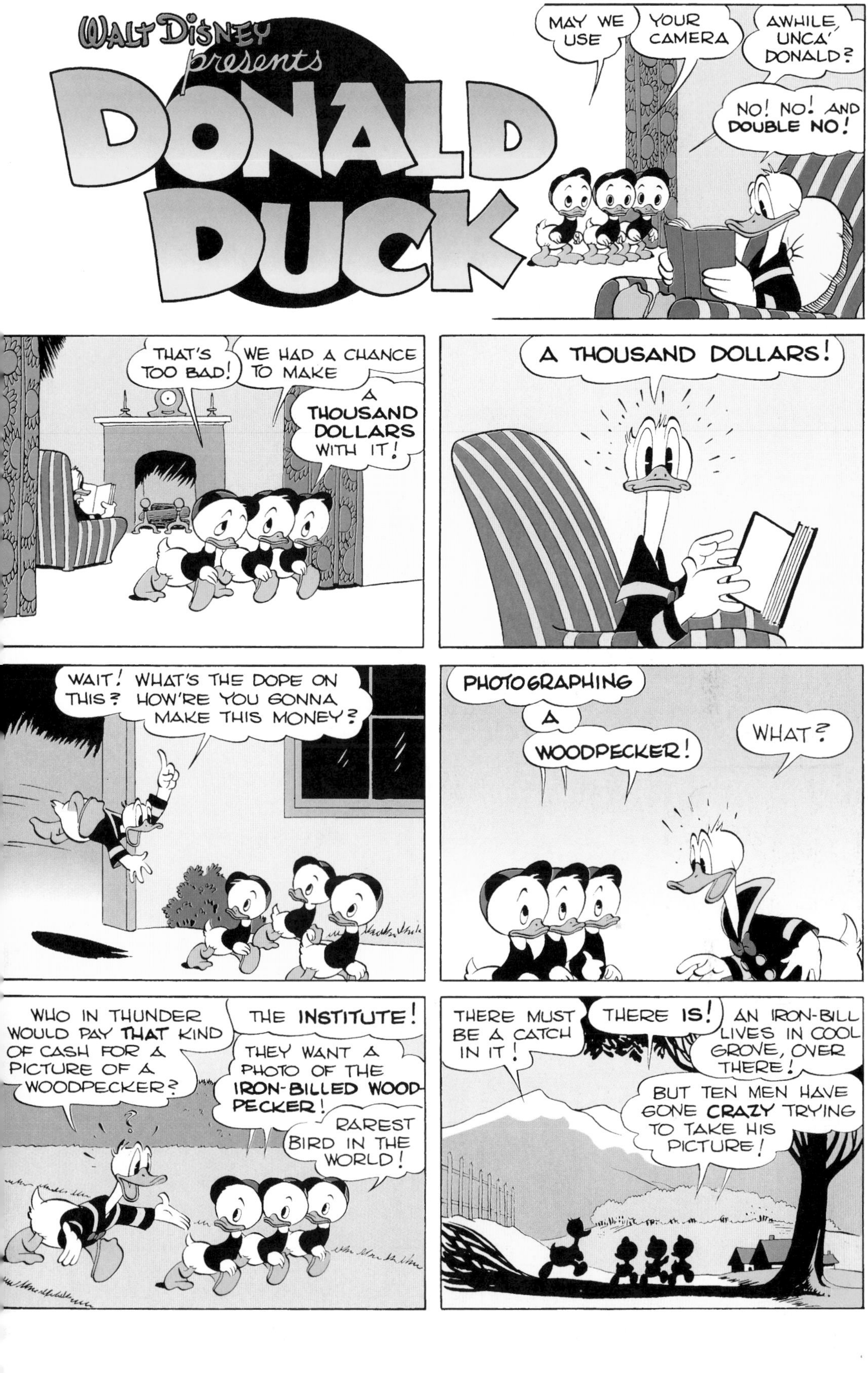
WALT DISNEY presents
DONALD DUCK
MAY WE USE
YOUR CAMERA
AWHILE, UNCA' DONALD?
NO! NO! AND DOUBLE NO!
THAT'S TOO BAD!
WE HAD A CHANCE TO MAKE
A THOUSAND DOLLARS WITH IT!
A THOUSAND DOLLARS!
WAIT! WHAT'S THE DOPE ON THIS? HOW'RE YOU GONNA MAKE THIS MONEY?
PHOTOGRAPHING
A
WOODPECKER!
WHAT?
WHO IN THUNDER WOULD PAY THAT KIND OF CASH FOR A PICTURE OF A WOODPECKER?
THE INSTITUTE!
THEY WANT A PHOTO OF THE IRON-BILLED WOODPECKER!
RAREST BIRD IN THE WORLD!
THERE MUST BE A CATCH IN IT!
THERE IS!
AN IRON-BILL LIVES IN COOL GROVE, OVER THERE!
BUT TEN MEN HAVE GONE CRAZY TRYING TO TAKE HIS PICTURE!

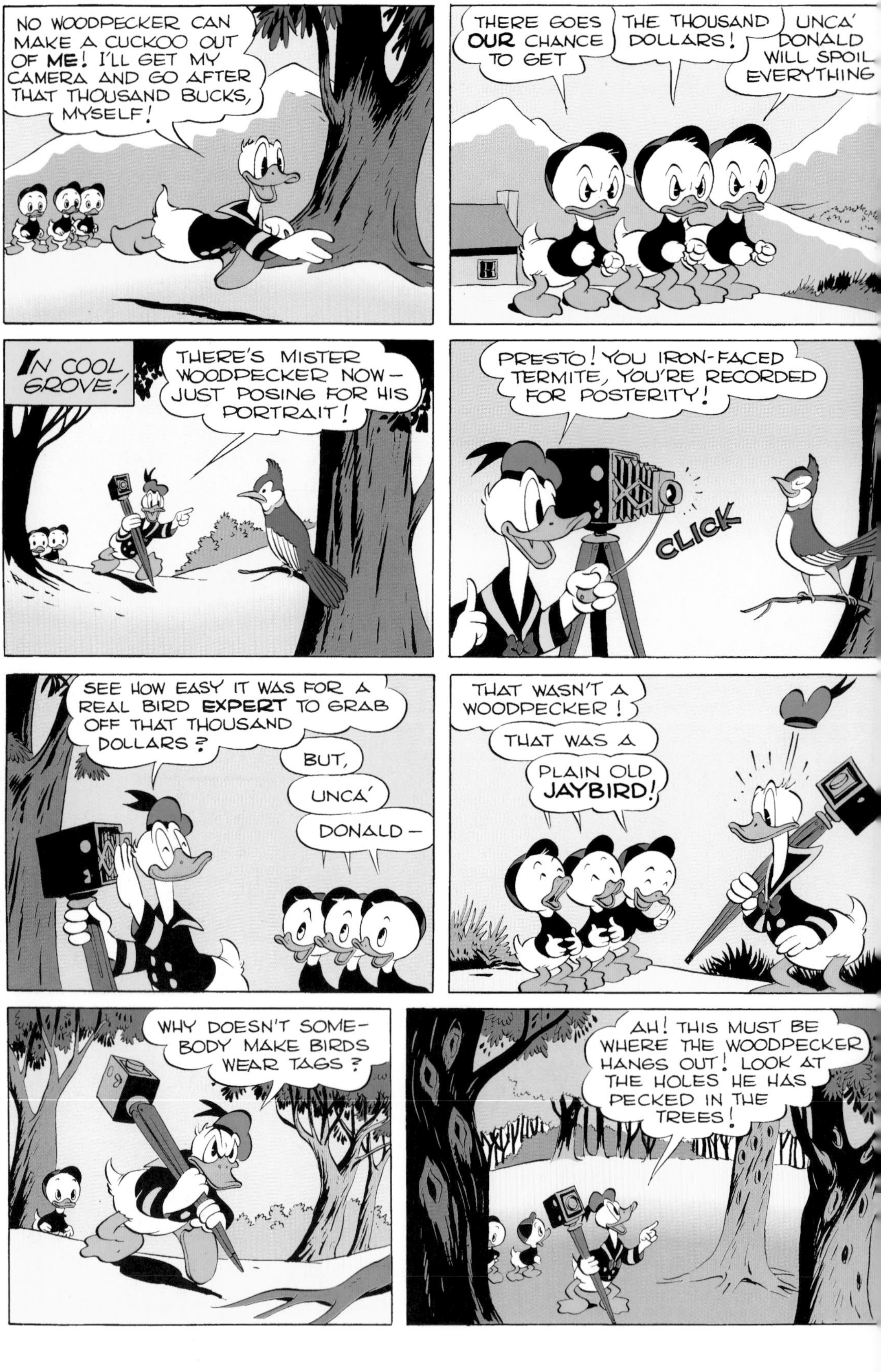
NO WOODPECKER CAN MAKE A CUCKOO OUT OF **ME**! I'LL GET MY CAMERA AND GO AFTER THAT THOUSAND BUCKS, MYSELF!
THERE GOES **OUR** CHANCE TO GET
THE THOUSAND DOLLARS!
UNCA' DONALD WILL SPOIL EVERYTHING
IN COOL GROVE!
THERE'S MISTER WOODPECKER NOW— JUST POSING FOR HIS PORTRAIT!
PRESTO! YOU IRON-FACED TERMITE, YOU'RE RECORDED FOR POSTERITY!
CLICK
SEE HOW EASY IT WAS FOR A REAL BIRD **EXPERT** TO GRAB OFF THAT THOUSAND DOLLARS?
BUT,
UNCA'
DONALD—
THAT WASN'T A WOODPECKER!
THAT WAS A
PLAIN OLD **JAYBIRD**!
WHY DOESN'T SOMEBODY MAKE BIRDS WEAR TAGS?
AH! THIS MUST BE WHERE THE WOODPECKER HANGS OUT! LOOK AT THE HOLES HE HAS PECKED IN THE TREES!

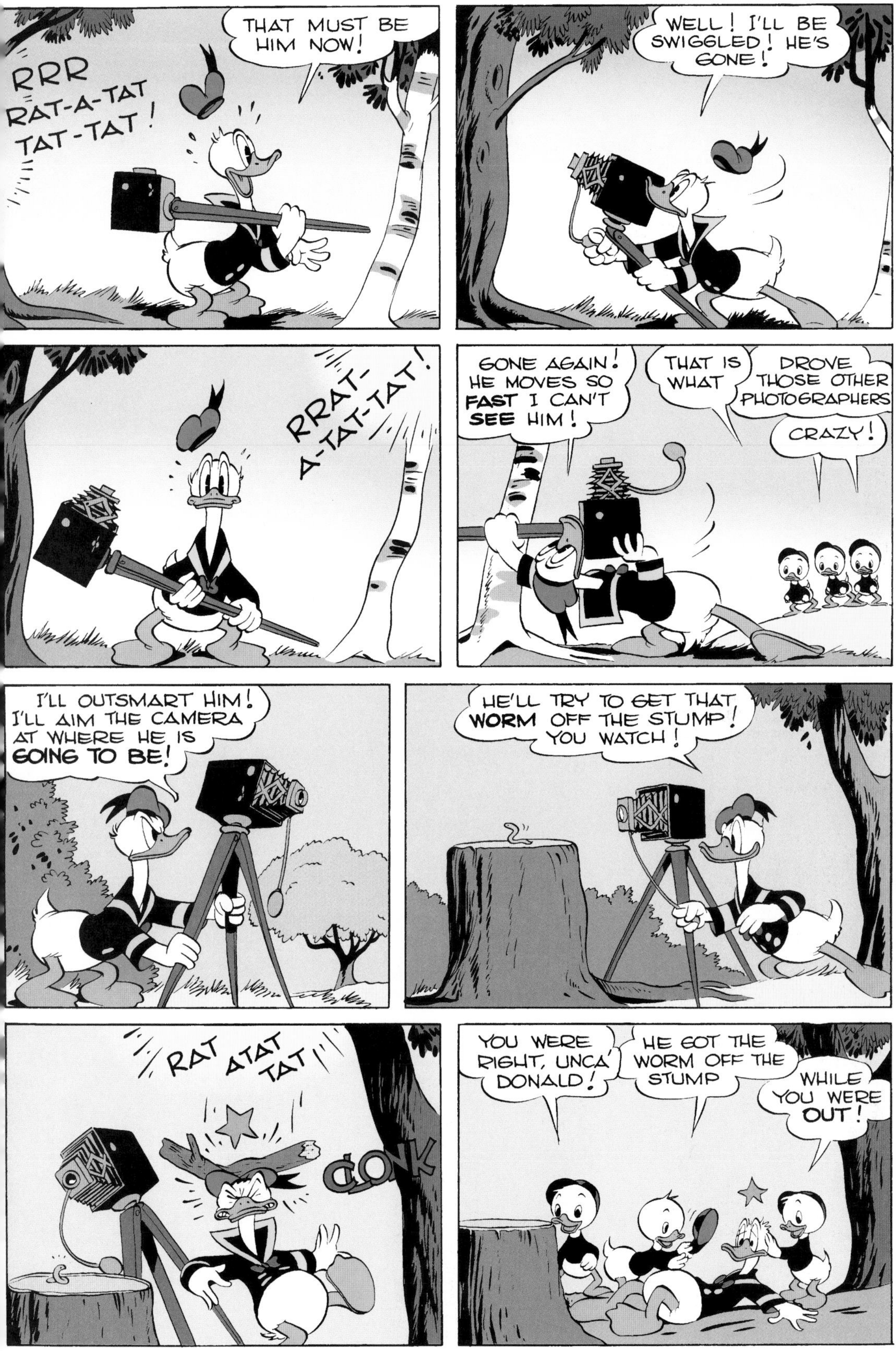
THAT MUST BE HIM NOW!
RRR RAT-A-TAT TAT-TAT!
WELL! I'LL BE SWIGGLED! HE'S GONE!
RRAT-A-TAT-TAT!
GONE AGAIN! HE MOVES SO FAST I CAN'T SEE HIM!
THAT IS WHAT
DROVE THOSE OTHER PHOTOGRAPHERS
CRAZY!
I'LL OUTSMART HIM! I'LL AIM THE CAMERA AT WHERE HE IS GOING TO BE!
HE'LL TRY TO GET THAT WORM OFF THE STUMP! YOU WATCH!
RAT ATAT TAT
CLONK
YOU WERE RIGHT, UNCA' DONALD!
HE GOT THE WORM OFF THE STUMP
WHILE YOU WERE OUT!

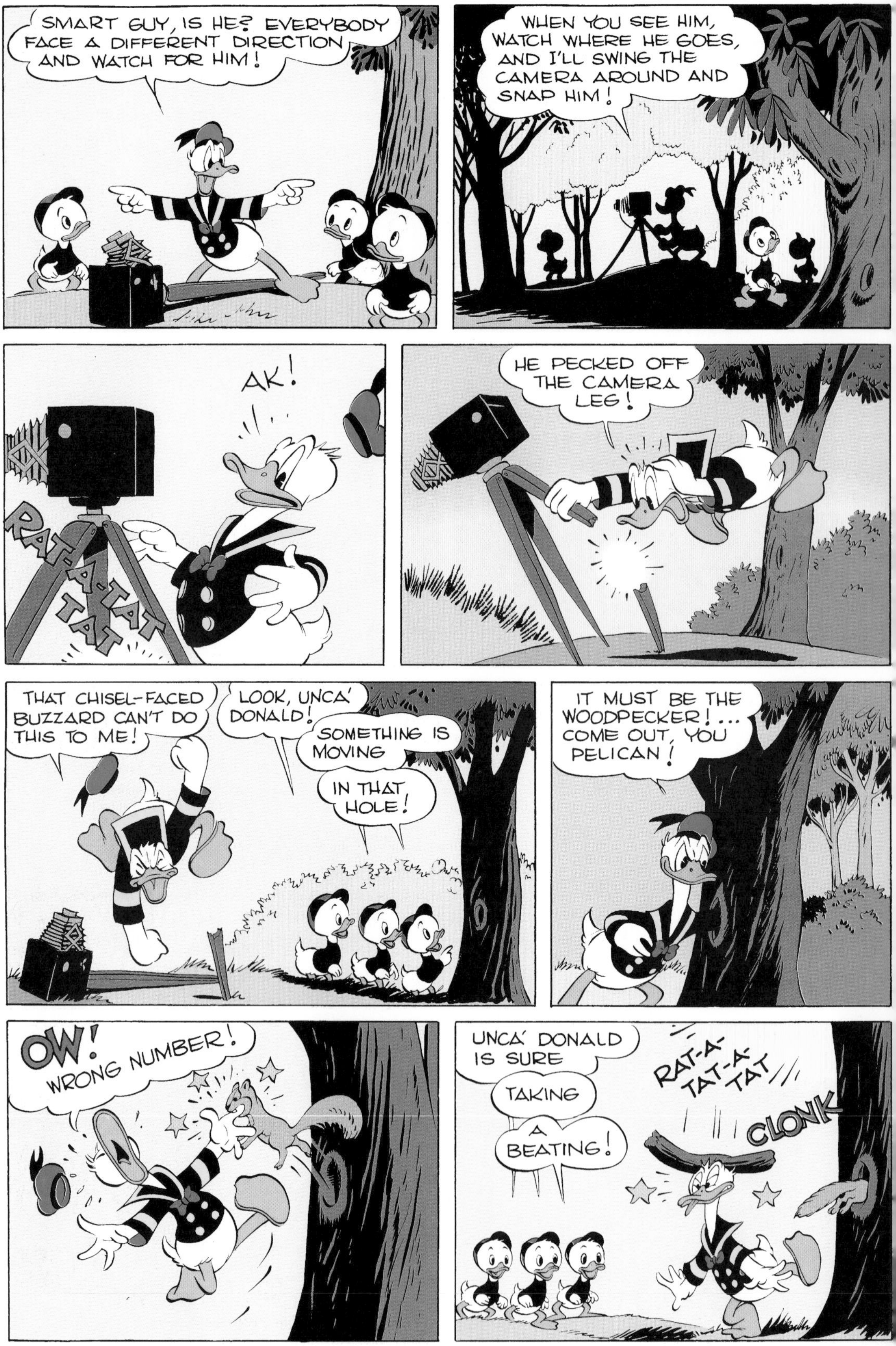

SMART GUY, IS HE? EVERYBODY FACE A DIFFERENT DIRECTION AND WATCH FOR HIM!
WHEN YOU SEE HIM, WATCH WHERE HE GOES, AND I'LL SWING THE CAMERA AROUND AND SNAP HIM!
AK!
RAT-A-TAT TAT
HE PECKED OFF THE CAMERA LEG!
THAT CHISEL-FACED BUZZARD CAN'T DO THIS TO ME!
LOOK, UNCA' DONALD!
SOMETHING IS MOVING
IN THAT HOLE!
IT MUST BE THE WOODPECKER!... COME OUT, YOU PELICAN!
OW! WRONG NUMBER!
UNCA' DONALD IS SURE
TAKING
A BEATING!
RAT-A-TAT-A-TAT
CLONK

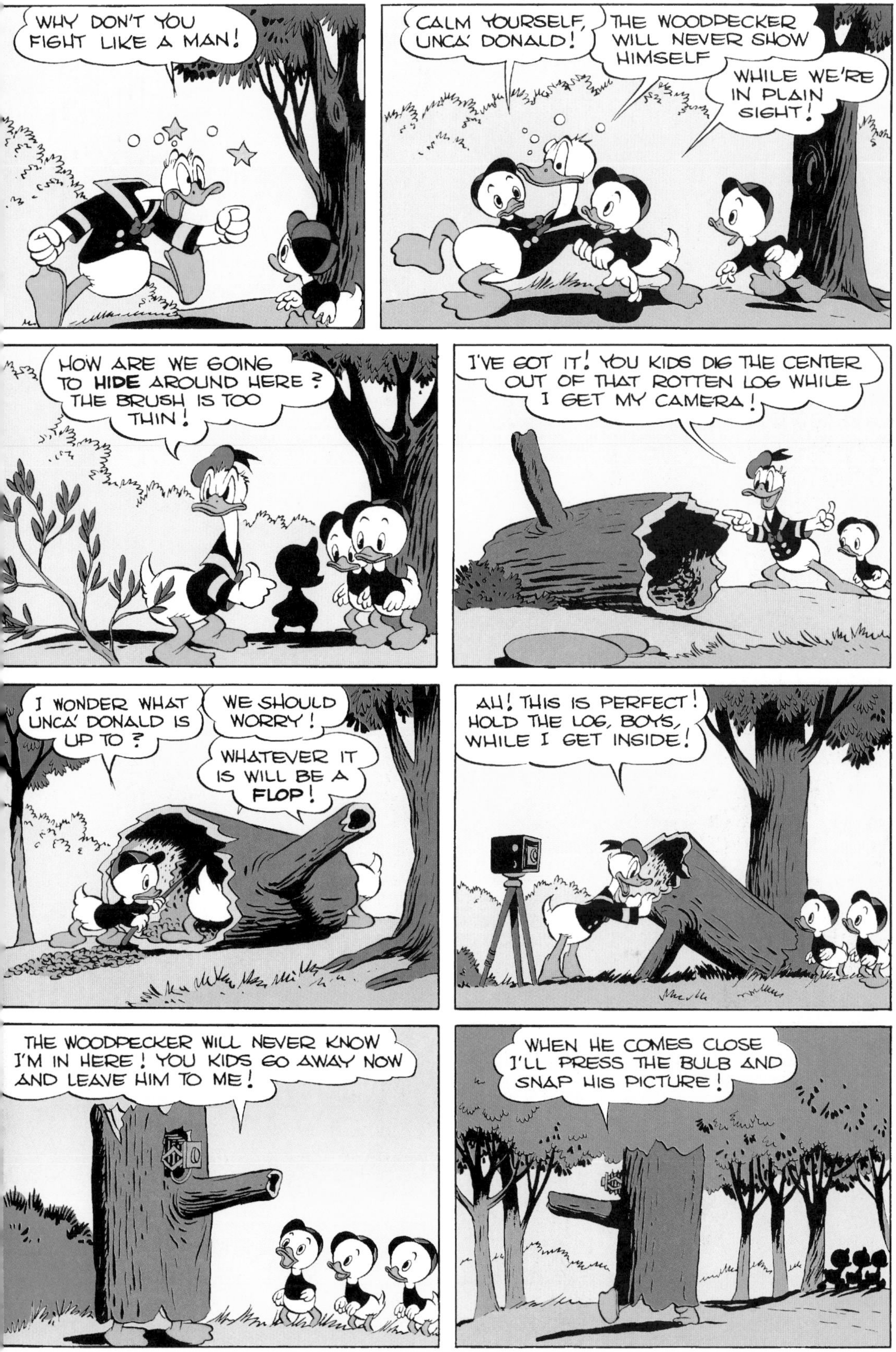
WHY DON'T YOU FIGHT LIKE A MAN!
CALM YOURSELF, UNCA' DONALD!
THE WOODPECKER WILL NEVER SHOW HIMSELF
WHILE WE'RE IN PLAIN SIGHT!
HOW ARE WE GOING TO HIDE AROUND HERE? THE BRUSH IS TOO THIN!
I'VE GOT IT! YOU KIDS DIG THE CENTER OUT OF THAT ROTTEN LOG WHILE I GET MY CAMERA!
I WONDER WHAT UNCA' DONALD IS UP TO?
WE SHOULD WORRY!
WHATEVER IT IS WILL BE A FLOP!
AH! THIS IS PERFECT! HOLD THE LOG, BOYS, WHILE I GET INSIDE!
THE WOODPECKER WILL NEVER KNOW I'M IN HERE! YOU KIDS GO AWAY NOW AND LEAVE HIM TO ME!
WHEN HE COMES CLOSE I'LL PRESS THE BULB AND SNAP HIS PICTURE!

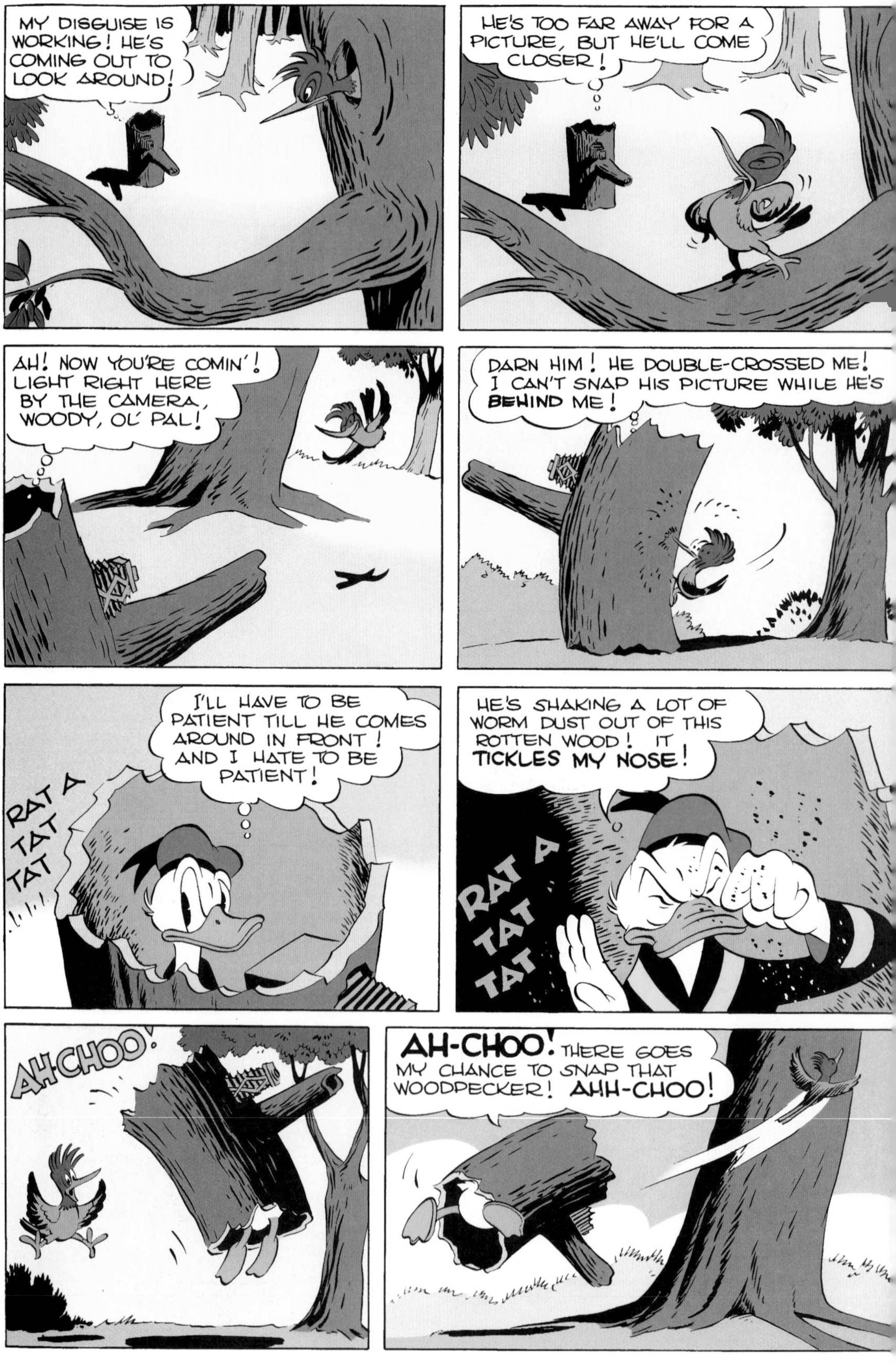
MY DISGUISE IS WORKING! HE'S COMING OUT TO LOOK AROUND!
HE'S TOO FAR AWAY FOR A PICTURE, BUT HE'LL COME CLOSER!
AH! NOW YOU'RE COMIN'! LIGHT RIGHT HERE BY THE CAMERA, WOODY, OL' PAL!
DARN HIM! HE DOUBLE-CROSSED ME! I CAN'T SNAP HIS PICTURE WHILE HE'S BEHIND ME!
RAT A TAT TAT
I'LL HAVE TO BE PATIENT TILL HE COMES AROUND IN FRONT! AND I HATE TO BE PATIENT!
HE'S SHAKING A LOT OF WORM DUST OUT OF THIS ROTTEN WOOD! IT TICKLES MY NOSE!
RAT A TAT TAT
AH-CHOO!
AH-CHOO! THERE GOES MY CHANCE TO SNAP THAT WOODPECKER! AHH-CHOO!

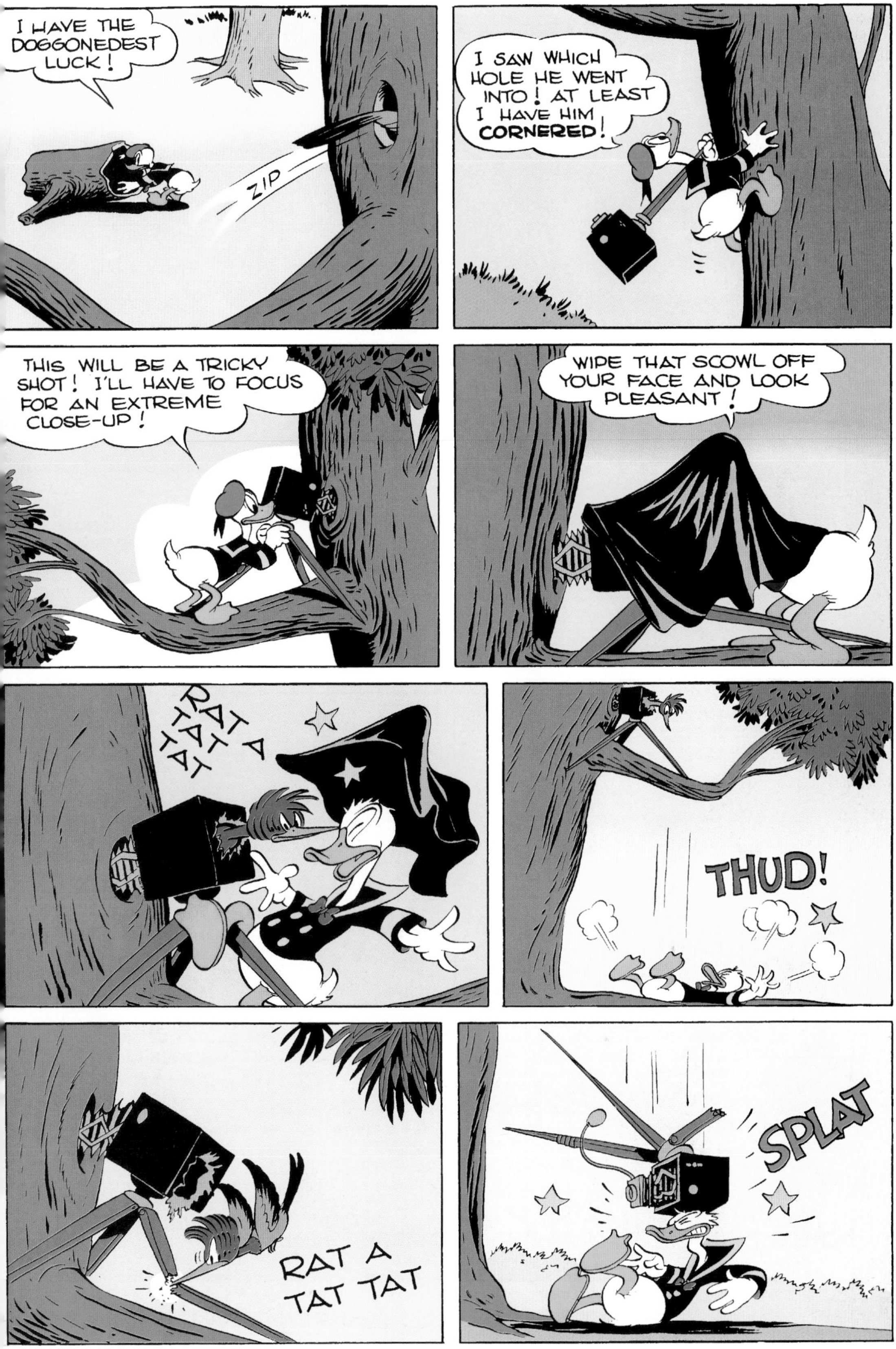
I HAVE THE DOGGONEDEST LUCK!
ZIP
I SAW WHICH HOLE HE WENT INTO! AT LEAST I HAVE HIM **CORNERED**!
THIS WILL BE A TRICKY SHOT! I'LL HAVE TO FOCUS FOR AN EXTREME CLOSE-UP!
WIPE THAT SCOWL OFF YOUR FACE AND LOOK PLEASANT!
RAT A TAT TAT
THUD!
RAT A TAT TAT
SPLAT

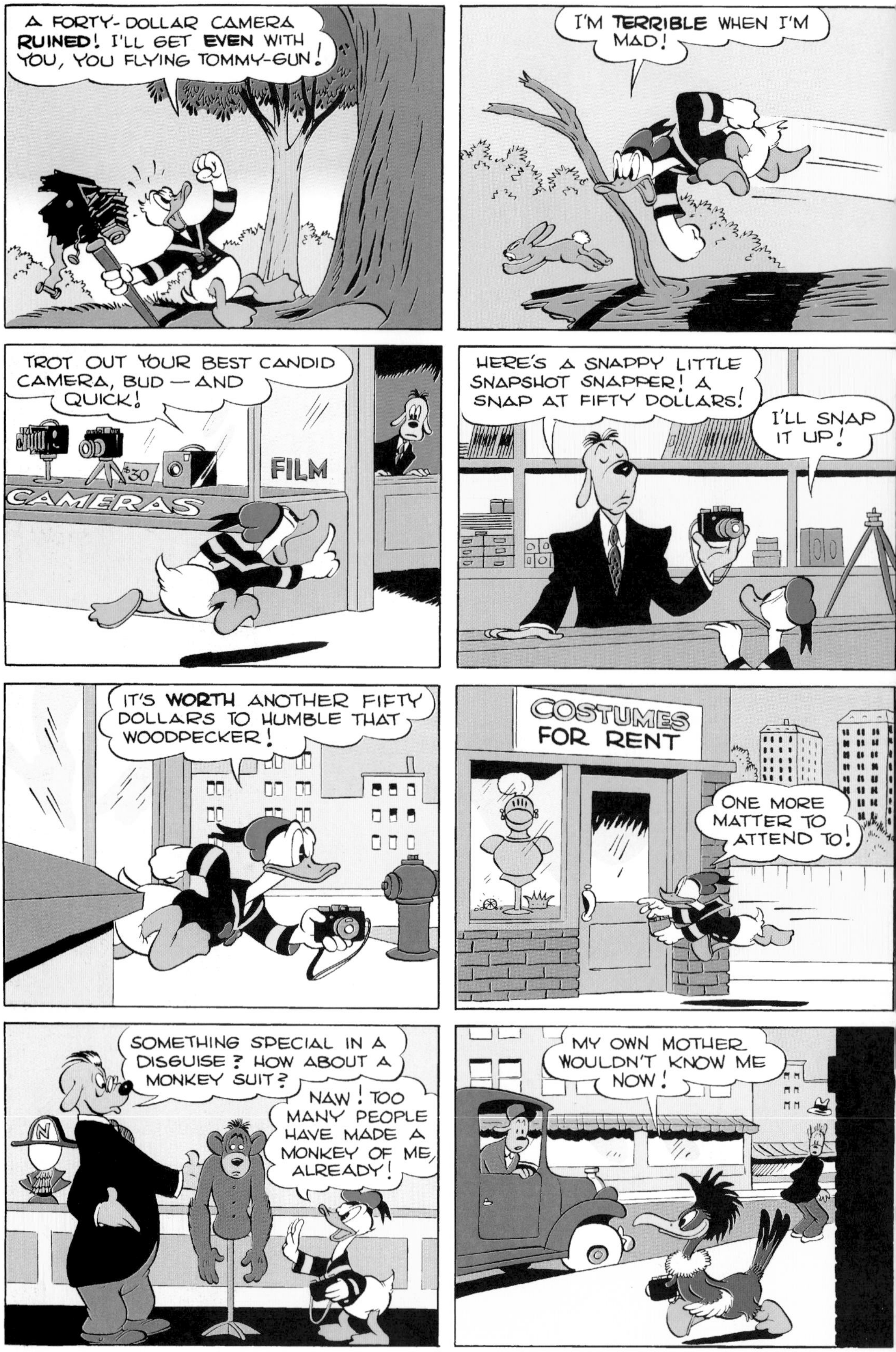
A FORTY-DOLLAR CAMERA **RUINED**! I'LL GET **EVEN** WITH YOU, YOU FLYING TOMMY-GUN!
I'M **TERRIBLE** WHEN I'M MAD!
TROT OUT YOUR BEST CANDID CAMERA, BUD — AND QUICK!
$30
FILM
CAMERAS
HERE'S A SNAPPY LITTLE SNAPSHOT SNAPPER! A SNAP AT FIFTY DOLLARS!
I'LL SNAP IT UP!
IT'S **WORTH** ANOTHER FIFTY DOLLARS TO HUMBLE THAT WOODPECKER!
COSTUMES FOR RENT
ONE MORE MATTER TO ATTEND TO!
SOMETHING SPECIAL IN A DISGUISE? HOW ABOUT A MONKEY SUIT?
NAW! TOO MANY PEOPLE HAVE MADE A MONKEY OF ME ALREADY!
MY OWN MOTHER WOULDN'T KNOW ME NOW!

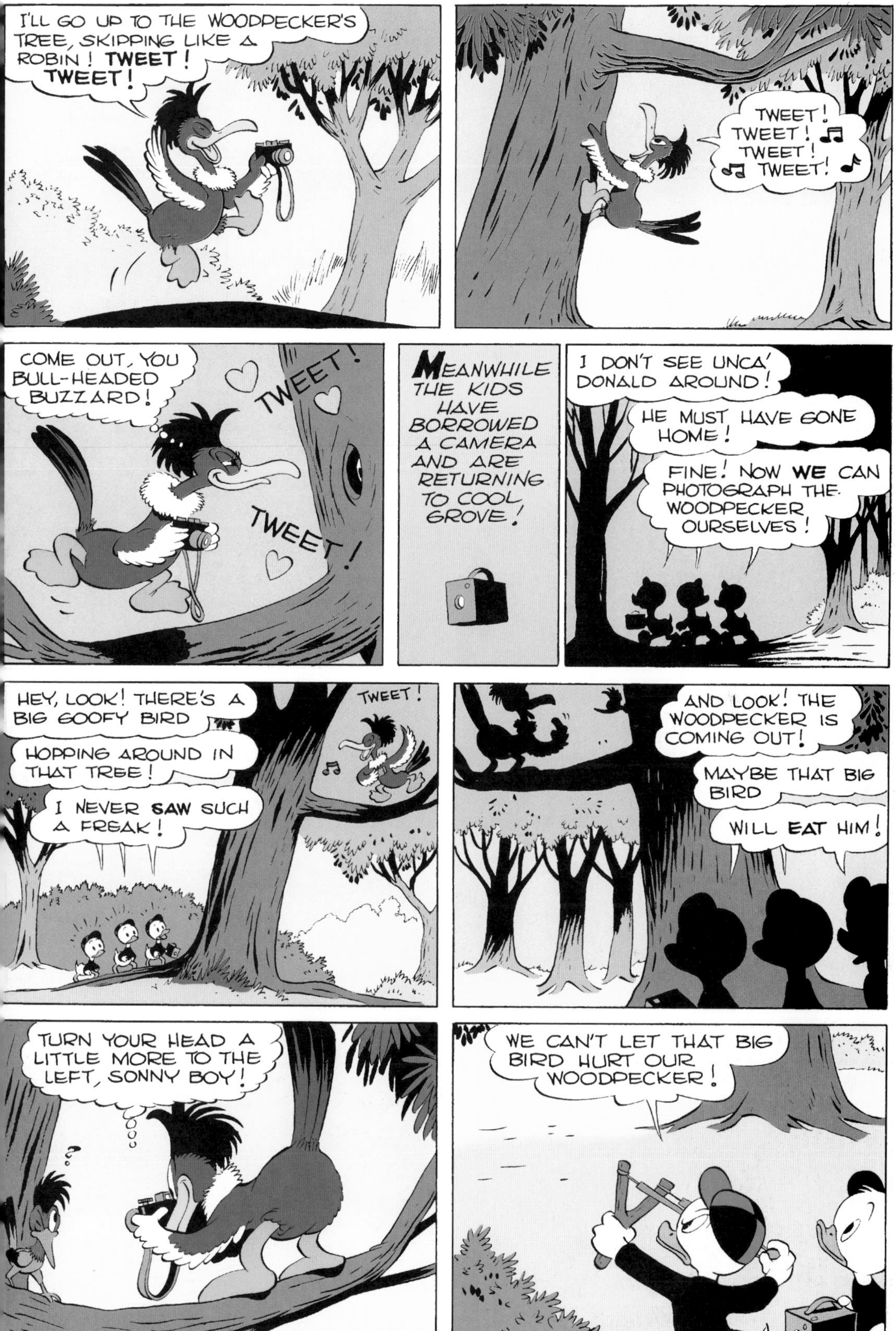
I'LL GO UP TO THE WOODPECKER'S TREE, SKIPPING LIKE A ROBIN! TWEET! TWEET!
TWEET! TWEET! TWEET! TWEET!
COME OUT, YOU BULL-HEADED BUZZARD!
TWEET!
TWEET!
MEANWHILE THE KIDS HAVE BORROWED A CAMERA AND ARE RETURNING TO COOL GROVE!
I DON'T SEE UNCA' DONALD AROUND!
HE MUST HAVE GONE HOME!
FINE! NOW WE CAN PHOTOGRAPH THE WOODPECKER OURSELVES!
HEY, LOOK! THERE'S A BIG GOOFY BIRD
HOPPING AROUND IN THAT TREE!
I NEVER SAW SUCH A FREAK!
TWEET!
AND LOOK! THE WOODPECKER IS COMING OUT!
MAYBE THAT BIG BIRD
WILL EAT HIM!
TURN YOUR HEAD A LITTLE MORE TO THE LEFT, SONNY BOY!
WE CAN'T LET THAT BIG BIRD HURT OUR WOODPECKER!

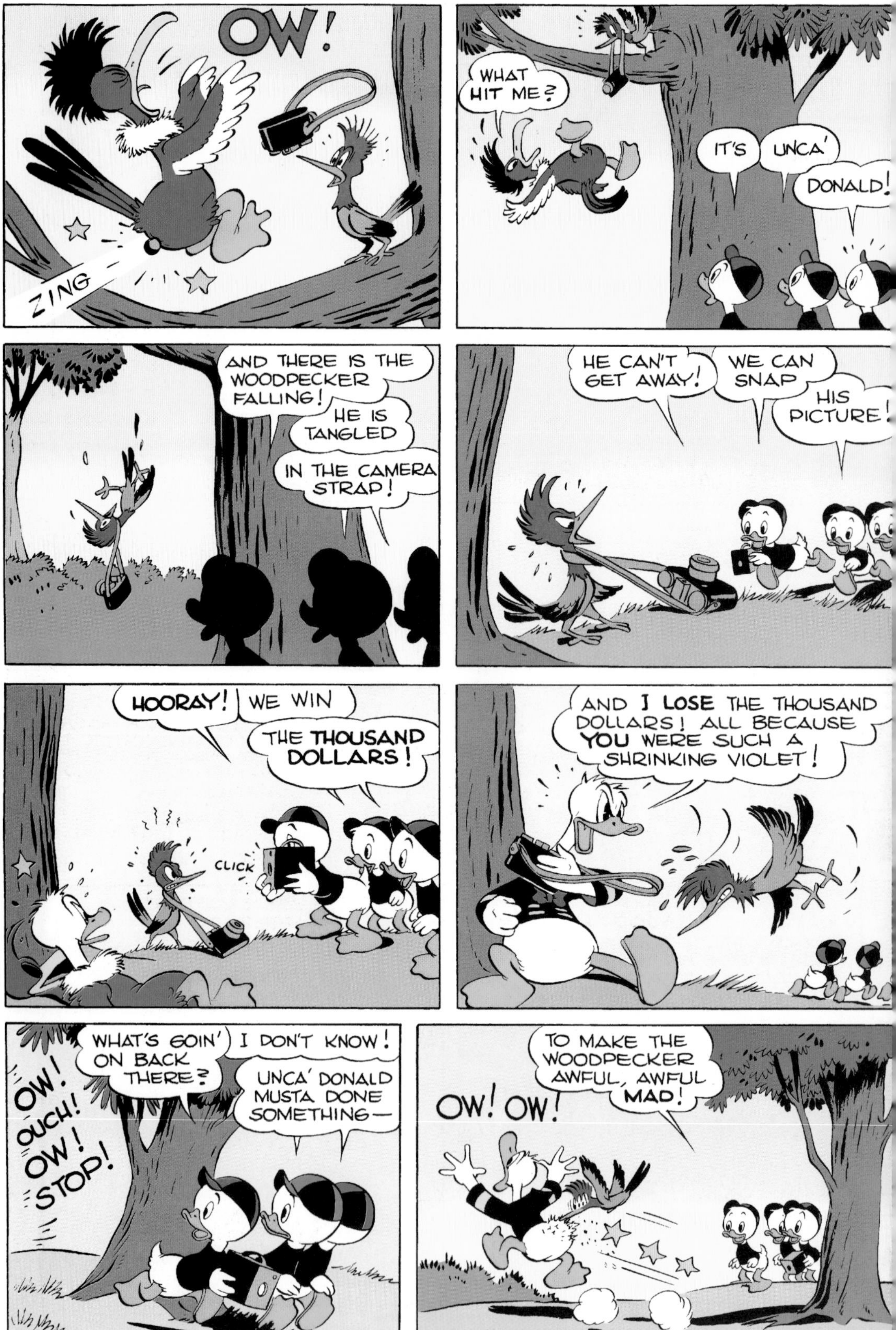
OW!
ZING
WHAT HIT ME?
IT'S
UNCA'
DONALD!
AND THERE IS THE WOODPECKER FALLING!
HE IS TANGLED
IN THE CAMERA STRAP!
HE CAN'T GET AWAY!
WE CAN SNAP
HIS PICTURE!
HOORAY!
WE WIN
THE THOUSAND DOLLARS!
CLICK
AND I LOSE THE THOUSAND DOLLARS! ALL BECAUSE YOU WERE SUCH A SHRINKING VIOLET!
OW! OUCH! OW! STOP!
WHAT'S GOIN' ON BACK THERE?
I DON'T KNOW!
UNCA' DONALD MUSTA DONE SOMETHING—
OW! OW!
TO MAKE THE WOODPECKER AWFUL, AWFUL MAD!

Walt Disney's

Fethry Duck

Shell Game

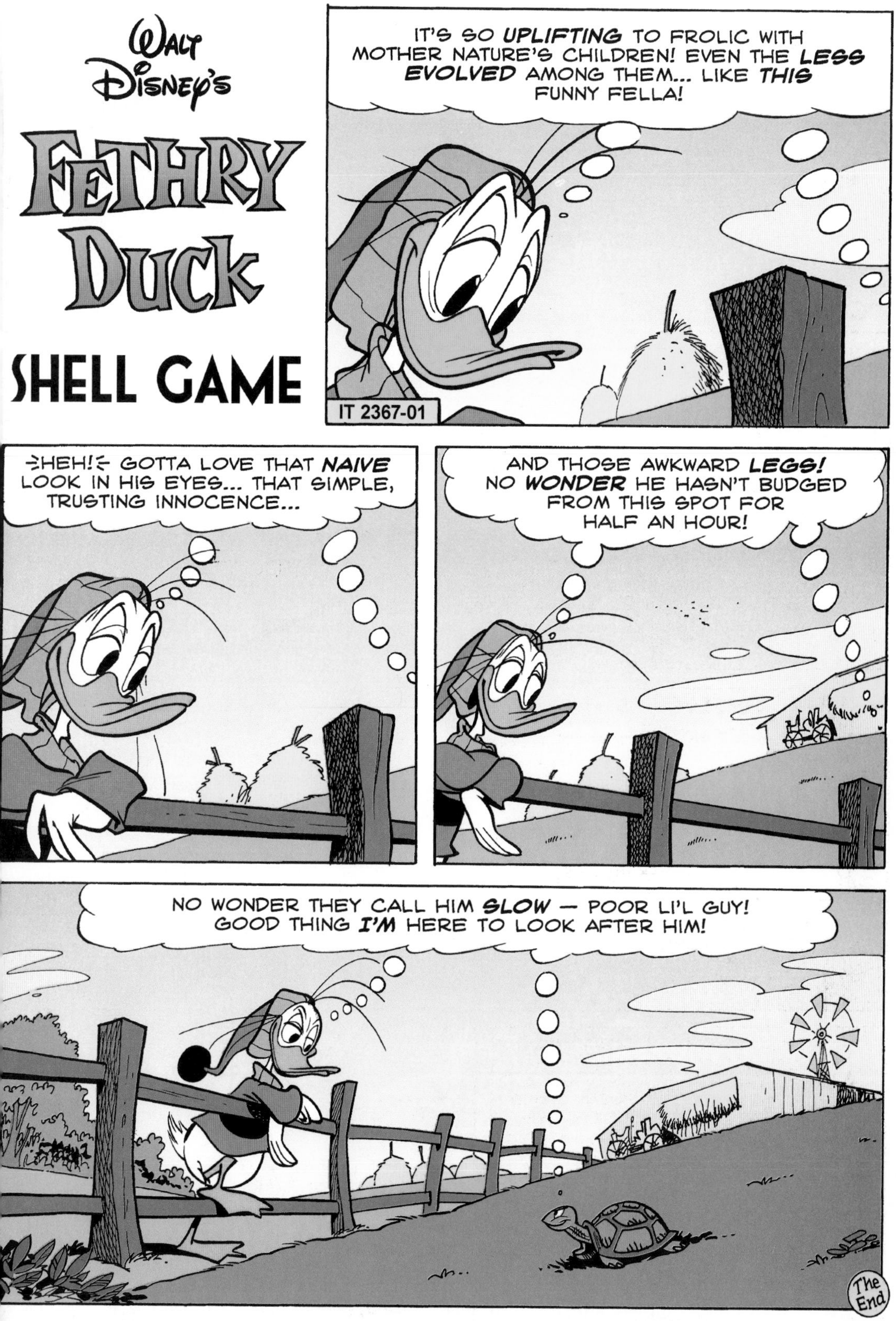
IT'S SO UPLIFTING TO FROLIC WITH MOTHER NATURE'S CHILDREN! EVEN THE LESS EVOLVED AMONG THEM... LIKE THIS FUNNY FELLA!
IT 2367-01
HEH! GOTTA LOVE THAT NAIVE LOOK IN HIS EYES... THAT SIMPLE, TRUSTING INNOCENCE...
AND THOSE AWKWARD LEGS! NO WONDER HE HASN'T BUDGED FROM THIS SPOT FOR HALF AN HOUR!
NO WONDER THEY CALL HIM SLOW — POOR LI'L GUY! GOOD THING I'M HERE TO LOOK AFTER HIM!
The End

Gemstone Publishing presents

More Life and Times of $crooge McDuck

Walt Disney's
Gemstone
The Life and Times of
$crooge McDuck
Companion
by
DON ROSA

You asked for them, and here they are... the prequels, the sequels, and the in-between-quels to Don Rosa's *Life and Times of Scrooge McDuck!* Filling in the gaps between the twelve original chapters are "The Cowboy Captain of the Cutty Sark" (Chapter 3B/*Uncle Scrooge* 318), "The Vigilante of Pizen Bluff" (Chapter 6B/*US* 306), "The Prisoner of White Agony Creek" (the all-new Chapter 8B!), "Hearts of the Yukon" (Chapter 8C/*Walt Disney Giant* 1) and "The Sharpie of the Culebra Cut" (Chapter 10B/*US* 332).

But wait... there's more! We've got Don's first look at Scrooge's youth—the famous flashback from "Last Sled to Dawson" (*Uncle Scrooge Adventures* 5). We've got the apocrypha: "Of Ducks and Dimes and Destinies" (Chapter 0/*US* 297) and "The Dream of a Lifetime!" (*US* 329), with the modern-day Magica De Spell and Beagle Boys wreaking havoc in Scrooge's past. And we've got the commentary—more than a dozen pages of Rosa recollections on how these classics came to be, all for only $16.99!

STILL ON SALE (AT A TIGHTWAD-FRIENDLY PRICE!)

It's Rosa's original twelve-chapter quest into Scrooge's life—presented in a 264-page volume replete with extensive authorial commentary. From Scrooge's Scottish childhood to his worldwide quest for gold; from his ill-starred romances to his meetings with history's heroes, this classic biography marked a milestone in duck comics. Annotated by Rosa himself and full of new-to-North-America art, Gemstone's $16.99 collected edition belongs on every Disney fan's bookshelf.

Gemstone Publishing

Walt Disney's
The Life and Times of
$crooge McDuck
by
DON ROSA

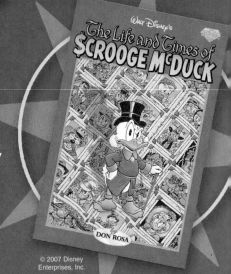

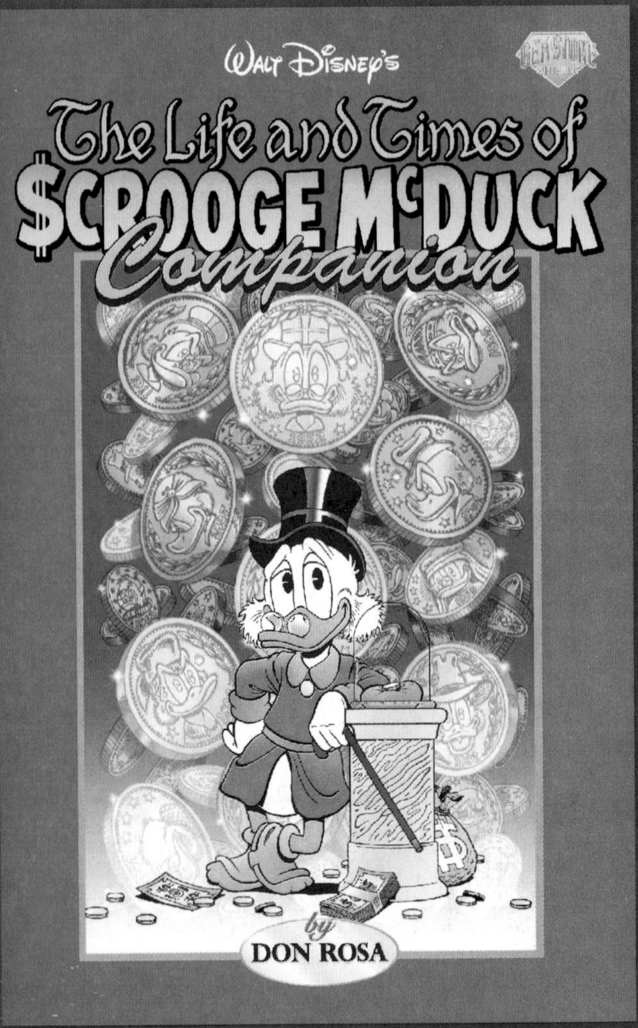